Global Corporate Identity

The Cross-Border Marketing Challenge

Murray J. Lubliner

Rockport Publishers, Inc.
Distributed by North Light Books
Cincinnati, Ohio

First published in the United States of America by:
Rockport Publishers, Inc. 146 Granite Street Rockport, Massachusetts 01966
Telephone: (508) 546-9590 Fax: (508) 546-7141 Telex: 5106019284 ROCKORT PUB

Distributed to the book trade and art trade in the U.S. and Canada by:
North Light, an imprint of F & W Publications 1507 Dana Avenue Cincinnati, Ohio 45207
Telephone: (513) 531-2222

Other Distribution by:
Rockport Publishers, Inc. Rockport, Massachusetts 01966

ISBN 1-56496-110-9

10 9 8 7 6 5 4 3 2 1

Project Director: Murray J. Lubliner
Designer: Cardinal Inc.
Editor: Rosalie Grattaroti
Production Manager: Barbara States
Production Assistant: Pat O'Maley

Printed in Hong Kong

CONTENTS

I N T R O D U C T I O N

Corporate Identity, conceived fifty years ago as a concept to help companies communicate accurate images of their attributes and businesses, requires rethinking to meet the challenges of globalization.

"As competition for recognition becomes more intense, identity planning offers a company an efficient and cost-effective opportunity to build awareness, strengthen market position, and communicate to diverse audiences. Companies must look beyond their own borders when developing identity strategies. Specific markets and changing conditions may require modifications in identity practices within the framework of the basic system. The goal is to differentiate and distinguish a company from all the others. Therefore, an effective identity posture cuts across cultures and languages.

The companies represented in this book, such as Texaco, Gillette, Dow Chemical, Heinz, KFC and Continental Airlines, are global marketers. They understand that an identity program must be consistent yet flexible to shape their corporate images in worldwide markets.

The world can no longer be viewed as one homogenous bazaar in which corporate identity is applied indiscriminately. To profit from optimum communications and marketing support, an identity policy should be planned both from a strategic point-of-view - as an asset that ensures synergistic payback for the long-term, and as a vehicle with built-in flexibility that allows quick response to changing conditions in a market.

How to strengthen name recognition is essential. A company name that is well- known in its own markets may have little or no awareness in other markets. Some names "travel well" and are suitable for use globally. Other names may require modification or change because of cultural and linguistic characteristics. There is a tendency to combine names and logotypes in acquisition or merger situations, which result in cumbersome identities that are

difficult for people to understand. As a result, these names may be ignored by the very audiences towards whom the communications are directed.

It is crucial that name issues be resolved early in the business-combination process and viable alternatives evaluated. The objective always is to clearly articulate "who the company is" and "what it does". Each time a company acquires or merges, more names are added to the identity framework. The market equities in these names and reputations require careful analysis so their market strengths can be transferred not only to the new corporate entity but to all segments of the organization. "Words first," a foundation for sound identity planning, has become even more critical in a world in which there are no "foreigners," only people who communicate in foreign languages. Where there is a rationale for linking or combining names, an easily understood system of nomenclature relationships should be defined and in place before designers explore the visual opportunities for the identity. And, the designers should understand that what they are creating must be suitable for global applications.

On the following pages, you will be introduced to carefully selected identity programs for a diverse group of international companies that operate in a variety of business categories. Although marketing and image strategies may vary, each shares a common objective - to generate awareness, understanding and positive attitudes from their wide-ranging audiences.

— Murray J. Lubliner

Murray J. Lubliner has played a pivotal role in developing strategy-based communications and corporate identity systems for hundreds of companies throughout the world. He started his career at Lippincott & Margulies, where he had the opportunity to participate in the early development of Corporate Identity as a valuable management tool. For 17 years he was a partner in Lubliner/Saltz Inc., an identity and design consultancy. Currently, he is president of Murray J. Lubliner Associates in New York which specializes in strategic identity planning. He is a recognized authority in corporate identity, frequently contributes to business publications, and is an Adjunct Professor at New York University's Management Institute where he teaches "Identity, Image and the Bottom Line."

Addison Design Consultants

575 Sutter Street
San Francisco, California 94102
Tel: 415-956-7575
Fax: 415-433-8641

Addison was commissioned to transform the image of Britian's largest company, British Petroleum. The project provided a new look for more than 32,000 petrol stations around the world as well as hundreds of company vehicles. Ultimately, the design was extended to new kinds of service environments for the company's retail division which includes convenience stores, special day and overnight stops for truck drivers, and a business center.

▼ ▶

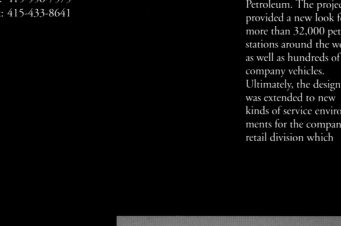

A ddison is an international, multi-cultural design consultancy with more than 200 specialists working from major cities throughout North America, Europe, and Asia.

Their expertise covers a wide range of disciplines — architecture, ergonomics, research and planning, name creation, graphic, industrial, and interior design.

The firm works with clients in all sectors of business to create and design identities, products, printed materials, packaging, and environments. They work in teams with a diverse range of skills and cultural backgrounds, thus ensuring that the ideas they develop are relevant to all the people their clients need to influence.

**Addison Design
Consultants**

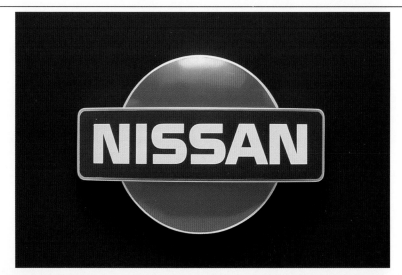

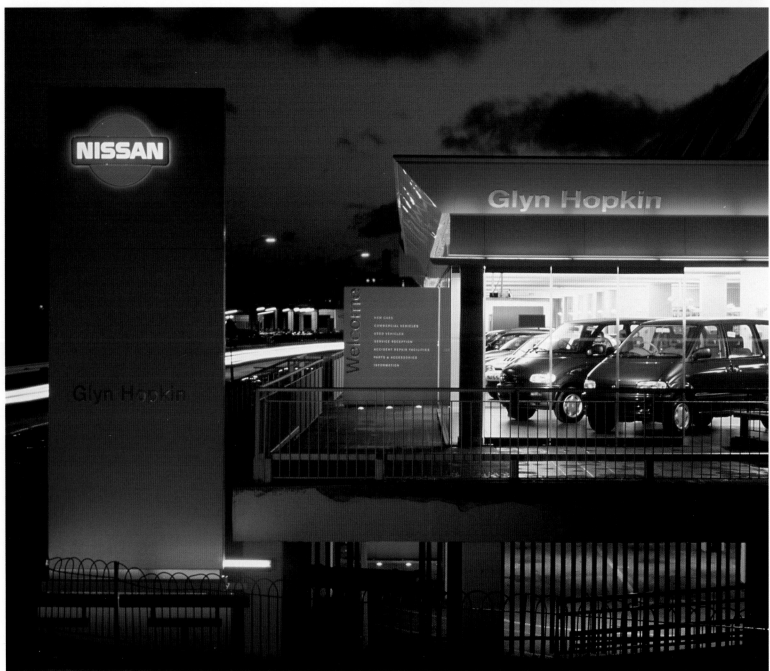

As a part of a bold new strategy enabling Nissan to differentiate itself as a leader amongst European volume car manufacturers, and to target a customer profile more appropriate to their product development, Addison was commissioned to develop a comprehensive redefinition of the retail brand in Europe. The objective was to create an appropriate yet differentiated retail identity for Nissan Europe's dealership network, both new-built and retrofit, which expressed its new market positioning and manifested it in every aspect of the dealership operation.

**Addison Design
Consultants**

As industry growth created opportunities for higher- and lower-priced chains, Holiday Inn recognized the need to expand. A segmentation strategy was recommended and names for three new hotel/motel chains were created: Crowne Plaza, Embassy Suites, and Hampton Inns. Addision developed the image of these new chains by creating their retail identities and applying them throughout the facility and all of its key media.

**Addison Design
Consultants**

Mitsukoshi is the oldest and most established department store in Japan. Its image was a store of fine tradition, but its lack of a progressive, innovative merchandising and marketing approach failed to attract a younger audience. Addison created a retail identity for the stores which signals a change in attitude toward its younger market and conveys a dynamic retail operation which capitalizes on Mitsukoshi's fine reputation.

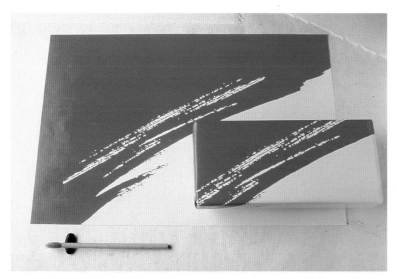

Anspach Grossman Portugal

711 Third Avenue
New York, NY 10017
Tel: 212-692-9000
Fax: 212-682-8376

Other location:
360 Post Street
San Francisco, CA 94108
Tel: 415-781-7337
Fax: 415-781-7346

Key clients:
American Express
Ameritech
Arthur Andersen & Co.
Citibank
Gillette
Hewlett-Packard
Kmart
MasterCard
  International
Mayo Clinic
MetLife
Mitsubishi Bank
National Australia
  Bank
New York Stock
  Exchange
Pfizer
Prudential Insurance
Quaker Oats
Raytheon
Sanyo
Sara Lee
Supervalu
Texaco
The BOC Group
Time Warner
Unisys
UPS

From left to right:

Joel Portugal,
Ken Love,
Gene Grossman,
Larry Ackerman,
Bill Schneider,
Ken Roberts

Helping companies undergo **change** is a key component of Anspach Grossman Portugal's expertise in identity consulting. Recognized for creating the identities of household brands, retail facilities, and major companies, one of the firm's most notable achievements is also its record for guiding some of the world's best-known corporations through periods of **transformation**. From classic renaming, **repositioning**, and branding situations to the communications challenges resulting from restructuring, re-engineering, partnering, and other mainstays of the multi-national business arena, Anspach Grossman Portugal applies its identity skills to clarify a company's image among all audiences.

The firm's hallmark is its team approach to consulting. With experience in multiple disciplines — management consulting, organizational psychology, **design**, architecture, brand management, linguistics, market **research**, and others — Anspach Grossman Portugal consultants can readily identify and understand the key dynamics of change. By tailoring practical communications solutions to address such issues as **misperception**, productivity, service quality, **culture**, competitive positioning, and **image**, the firm helps companies achieve a more accurate and **memorable** market presence.

**Anspach
Grossman
Portugal**

Behind every major cred-
it card is a sophisticated
marketing story involving
positioning, branding,
naming, and design. The
ultimate in corporate
packaging, credit cards
carry a hefty marketing
burden. Research by

Anspach Grossman
Portugal has found that
design can serve as a primary differentiator and
can also influence the fre-
quency of use. Each of
the cards here represents
a significant event — re-
positioning, new service

introduction, brand
extension — for the
sponsoring companies.

Clockwise, top five cards:
American Express green
corporate card, 1990;
Republic Bank gold and
green cards, 1993;

American Express
Optima card, 1992;
Texaco card, 1982.
Bottom three cards, left
to right: GE Rewards
card, 1992; Ameritech
Complete card, 1992;
American Express gold
corporate card, 1991.

How do you create brand awareness in a crowded retail gasoline market — and do it in one year?

That was the challenge when the West German utility acquired DeutscheTexaco in 1989 and agreed to drop the well-known Texaco brand. Searching for a memorable new retail identity led to a daring and innovative solution: Friendly imagery at the gas pump under the brand name, DEA, from the Latin word goddess. Applied to all marketing and advertising materials, rolling stock and retail facilities, DEA achieved extremely high levels of recognition and acceptance among the German public in record time. The most telling indicator of consumer acceptance, however, is in the numbers: Increases of 13% in gasoline sales and 15.5% in diesel fuel sales.

◀▼

**Anspach
Grossman
Portugal**

*"This is a different
company than before...
and we need a new face
to our various publics."*

With those words,
William L. Weiss, chair-
man and chief executive
officer of "Baby Bell"
Ameritech, unveiled its
new corporate identity in
1993, signaling the com-
pany's transformation
from a five-state geo-
graphic orientation to a
business built around

customers, with products
and services marketed
under a single brand
name — Ameritech.

A naming system also
developed by Anspach
Grossman Portugal unites
the company's 12 newly
reorganized market-
focused business units
under the Ameritech

name. The identity sys-
tem incorporates all visual communications of the
corporation — corporate
and marketing materials,
signage, vehicles, facilities, uniforms, and even
pay phones.

What's a true world-class brand? Just ask Gillette.

For the worldwide launch of the Sensor razor in 1989, Anspach Grossman Portugal developed a brand identity that became the foundation of a global mega-brand system that unites every product within the Gillette blade and razor line — including Sensor, Sensor for Women, SensorExcel, Atra, TracII, Foamy, and others — by a visual and verbal vocabulary. Centered on the powerful brand name, the system consistently links Gillette to sub-brands such as Sensor or Foamy. Graphic lock-up devices such as the wave and stripe graphic patterns, strong color, and proprietary typographic style combine to make the most of the Gillette brand image at the store level.

John Darman, business director for new products, blades, and razors, Gillette North Atlantic Group, states that "Gillette's mega-brand identity system lets us maintain consistent imagery throughout the world. New products can immediately capitalize on the recognition and credibility of the Gillette brand logo."

▼

**Anspach
Grossman
Portugal**

Interbrew, Europe's fourth largest beverage producer, was formed by the merger of two Belgian beer companies. Transforming Interbrew in 1991-1992 from a Belgian beer maker to an international, consumer-driven beverage company involved establishing the corporate brand through a broad-based identification system, a comprehensive corporate communications program, and a cultural change program which included developing a vision, mission, and new values in support of corporate strategy.

The design challenge that came from combining the two original companies — Artois and Piedboeuf — was to create a sense of corporate life that transcended the powerful brand identities which had been brought together under one roof.

Three different graphic concepts were developed: the first, a geometric "I" symbol to represent the new Interbrew, the second, a bottle cap as a metaphor for all beverages, and the third, a free-drawn glass to convey the idea of "a thirst for life," which became the unifying theme of a new corporate culture.

Of the three design directions, the Interbrew "I" established a clear sense of corporate identity while also becoming a humanizing element in support of the new culture.
▼

INTERBREW

interbrew

Interbrew

Sometimes even great global marketers have to relearn their own lessons. With each Texaco region operating autonomously instead of fostering a unified brand image, over time the independent management style led to dissonance and brand dilution.

The solution was "System 2000," a flexible concept designed to meet global needs into the 21st century that centers on Texaco's strong elements of brand equity. Updated and redesigned with a graphic "T" at its center, the modernized star symbol is at the core of the revitalized retail and brand identity. Drawing from a "family" of modules for convenience stores, car washes, gas bars, and auto service centers allows management to respond to varying market conditions. A comprehensive identity system incorporates all signage, packaging, promotional, and advertising media, and a naming system helps eliminate confusion at the pumps over gasoline options with generic names on color-coded dispensers. Texaco's dramatic 77.9% increase in gasoline sales at redesigned stations is evidence of System 2000's success.

▼

B.E.P. Design Group

Rue des Mimosas 44, B-1030 Brussels, Belgium
Tel: 32 2 215 34 00
Fax: 32 2 215 39 11

Corporate image, promotional material, stationery, and application manual for Credit Agricole, Belgian bank for suburbanites.

▼

Application of image for stationery.

 ▼ ▼

Logotype in three versions of language and configuration. Belgium is a multi-lingual country with French, Dutch, and German areas.

▲

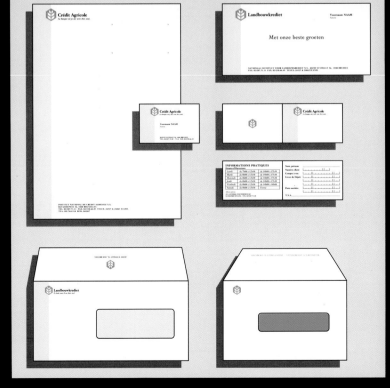

B.E.P. Design Group
building, close to the
center of Brussels.

▲ ▲

Jean J. Evrard and
Brigitte Evrard, principals
of B.E.P. Design Group

▲

Principals:
Brigitte Evrard
Jean J. Evrard
Year founded: 1976
Size of firm: 10
Key clients:
3M Europe
Assurity-Groupe
Victoire
Belgolaise Bank
Bic
Callataÿ & Wouters
Caisse Privée Banque
Crédit Agricole
Dieleman Gallery
Generale de Banque
Gervais Danone
Karlsberg
Kraftco
L'Oréal
Mc Cain Frima
Marabout
Nestlé
Reckitt & Colman,
Scott Paper Intl.
Soubry
Sky Shops
Brussels Airport
Vandemoortele
VAR
Wittamer

Today, without a well-conceived brand image and attractive packaging, even the best product has little chance of success. For B.E.P. Design Group, brand image and packaging have a vital role to play in positioning your product or your service as the number one choice for the consumer. B.E.P. Design Group owe their success to just the right combination of creativity and rigor, and to their never-ceasing analysis of market changes and new trends. Their method of analysis and conception covers all aspects of marketing strategy and all disciplines connected with brand image and packaging. The international and interdisciplinary team of B.E.P. Design Group are masters of both the most advanced computer design software and classic techniques. Since 1976, under the direction of Brigitte Evrard, B.E.P. Design Group has been creating packaging and brand images for prestigious international companies, as well as for renowned European and Belgian products and services.

**B.E.P. Design
Group**

Full range of products for
Karlsberg Brewery.
Established in 1878,
Karlsberg is one of
Germany's most impor-
tant breweries.

▼

Easy identification for the
consumer at the point of
sale.

▶

Different types of signage have been designed, as well as a significant number of promotional items including flags, umbrellas, ashtrays, billboards, stickers, glasses, trays, and clocks.

▼

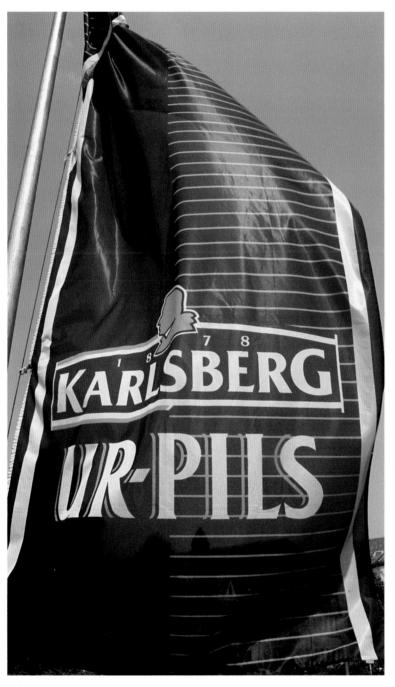

B.E.P. Design Group

The brewery has five different types of trucks, from the small delivery vehicle to the heavy-load truck.

▼

The Karlsberg image has been adapted for unusual situations on Europe's roads. This is a German bridge.

▲

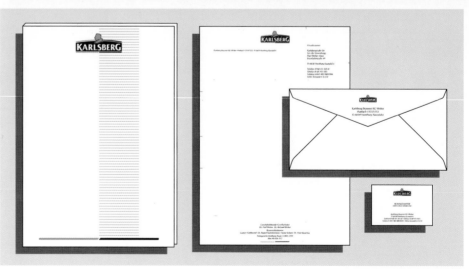

Application of the corporate identity on stationery.

▲

Application of a corp-
orate identity and the
developement of a
television spot and jingle
for V.A.R., an advertising
administration company.

▼

**B.E.P. Design
Group**

Corporate identity and
application for Sky Shops
of Brussels Airport.

A shopping bag provided
at Brussels Airport at
8:00 a.m. can be in
London at 9:00 a.m.,
Nairobi at 11:00 p.m.
and Los Angeles at 1:00
p.m. the same day.

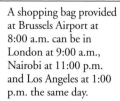

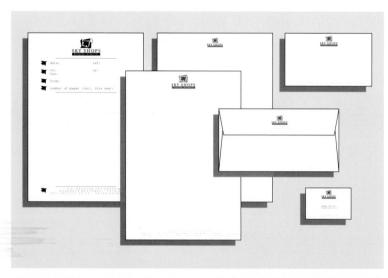

Coordination and
administration building.
The new Brussels Airport
is now in construction;
the design of new shops
is planned for 1994.

▶

Corporate identity for
Callatay & Wouters, a
consultancy involved in
computer network
architecture for banks
and insurance companies.

▼

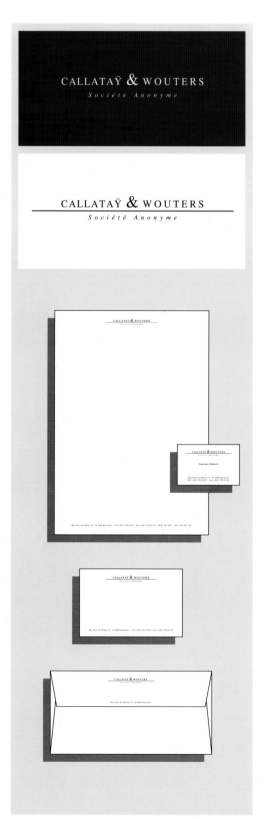

BrandEquity International
A Division of Selame Associates

2330 Washington Street
Newton, MA 02162
Tel: 617-969-0733
Fax: 617-969-1944
Mdm: 617-332-9076

Reprinted from
Global Corporate Identity.
Printed in Hong Kong.

A field of green helps identify Kmart's brand of home and garden products. KGro's carefully organized trade dress standards help the line to grow in an orderly manner, maintaining a quality perception while building brand equity.

▶

Introduced in the early eighties as the hottest new fitness product, Heavyhands packaging appealed instantly to its upscale target audience.

◀

The "W" brand identity and packaging trade dress project a winning image for Wilson Sporting Goods' numerous product lines.

▼

An international sports brand identity boosted General Sportcraft's quality product image and retail sales.

▶

"Penn's packaging catapulted the brand into the number one selling tennis ball within one year."

▼▶

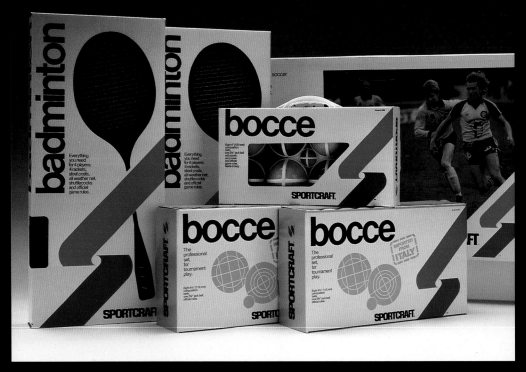

modifies existing designs to maximize brand performance.

BrandEquity International's team of marketing strategists, researchers, and design professionals partner with clients to ensure success in all aspects of program planning, development, and implementation. They are justifiably proud of their consistent record of achieving significant increases in brand awareness, sales, geographic distribution, and market share for their clients.

PRODUCTS BY **Kodak**

Kodak's advertising, brochure and exhibit design standards ensure both brand consistency and cost-effectiveness for the world's most recognized image maker.

◄

**BrandEquity
International**

Day or night, Store 24
clearly identifies New
England's largest conve-
nience store chain.
▶

In creating this retail
identity system for the
world leader in casual
wear, the objective was to
make Levi's Red an
instant identifier. The
retail branding and sign-
ing programs were devel-
oped concurrently with
the architecture in an
ideal collaboration of
professionals.

▲▶

Purity's retail identity projects an image of freshness and friendliness for this fast-growing regional supermarket chain.

◀

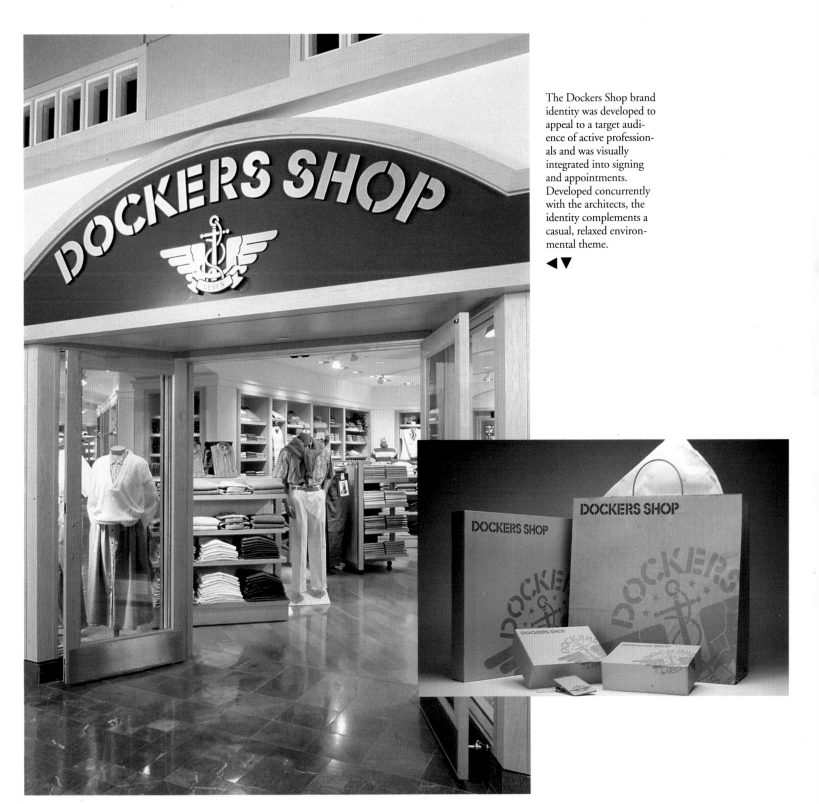

The Dockers Shop brand identity was developed to appeal to a target audience of active professionals and was visually integrated into signing and appointments. Developed concurrently with the architects, the identity complements a casual, relaxed environmental theme.

◀▼

BrandEquity International

Amoco Oil Company's Station of the Future achieves the distinction of identity stimulating architectural design. Two dynamic pylons serve as identifying supports for a span of solar mirrors reflecting the sky.

The Station of the Future was awarded the Environment Silver Medal by the Industrial Design Society of America. Note the original model.

Graphic creativity transforms the word "ultimate" into a powerful brand trademark for Amoco's premium synthetic motor oil.

For Pep Boys, one of the largest automotive aftermarket retailers in the United States, a custom typeface and banner graphic create an innovative retail identity for this industry leader.

►

Automotive Brands: World leaders in automotive aftermarketing rely on brand awareness to drive sales. An effective package does more than sell itself; it must also build long-term brand equity by maintaining and protecting brand and trade dress recognition among consumers at point-of-purchase.

◄

A "better-best" positioning for Champion's spark plug wire set packaging boosted sales by 86 per cent within six months of introduction.

◄

Digix is the name and identity we created for the Photo CD Division of Qualex, Inc., the world's largest photo finisher. The color bars of the trade dress represent the colors used in the digitizing process.

◄

Digix℠

For computer software manufacturer MapInfo, the corporate identity is also used as the product/ brand trade dress to reinforce recognition in a highly competitive category.

►

MapInfo® Desktop Mapping Software for Windows

MapBasic™ Desktop Mapping Tools

MapBasic™ Desktop Mapping Tools Reference

MapInfo® Desktop Mapping Software

MapInfo for Windows Getting Started

MapBasic™

MapBasic™ Desktop Mapping Tools User's Guide

Haworth, a leader in the design and manufacture of office furniture systems, uses its corporate signature as the foundation for unifying its divisions worldwide.

▼

HAWORTH

The 1st Impression name and brand identity the firm created enabled Avery-Dennison to introduce a high-end thermal binding system which complements desktop publishing systems. Success of the 1st Impression brand name prompted numerous line extensions for other Avery-Dennison office products.

►

1st Impression First Pack

1st Impression The Desktop Bindery™

1st Impression Covers

A billboard effect — created through Driscoll's brand identity applied to fresh strawberry cartons — maximizes consumer brand awareness in the supermarket environment while communicating product freshness.

▶

Veryfine's unique brand identity and package design catapulted this juice company's products into the largest-selling, single-serve brand at convenience stores in the United States.

◀

The Royal Cherry name and brand identity lifted the Oregon Cherry Grower's maraschino cherry products out of the commodity category and onto retail shelves internationally. Volume market share and geographic distribution increased 20 percent within two years.

◀

Bright & Associates

Identity and Design Consultants
901 Abbot Kinney Boulevard
Venice, California 90291
Tel: 310-450-2488
Fax: 310-452-1613

Corporate identity, naming, and packaging for Photo'go. This company introduced fast developing equipment for use in department and drug strores. Bright & Associates also created retail booths for in-store locations.

▼

Identity application to Marriot Host, the national airport food concession.

▼▼▼

Identity application to Photo'go rolling stock.

▼▼

Identity program encompassing stationery, signage, dealership environments, and all rolling stock for Ryder Transportation Services.

▼▶

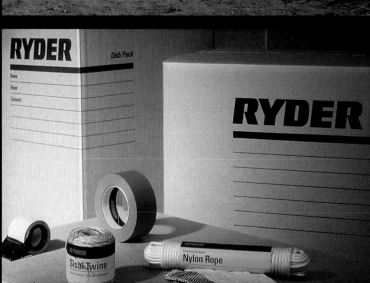

Corporate identity as displayed on signage for Coast Savings.

Brand identity and packaging for Darkseed computer game based on the drawings of H.R. Giger.

Corporate identity and signage application for EyeMasters stores.

Corporate identity and application for Wok Fast restaurants of California.

Bright & Associates

Corporate identity and application for Coast Savings.

Corporate identity and application for EyeMasters.

Bright and Associates is an international identity and design consulting firm founded in 1977 by Keith Bright, a leading figure in the design community for thirty years. Headquartered in Venice, California, Bright and Associates also has offices in Taiwan where they have been retained by the government as the leading consultant to plan and manage a five-year image enhancement program for the country and its major manufacturers.

Bright & Associates has successfully completed programs in a broad range of categories nationally and internationally. Services extend to naming, brand identity, corporate identity, packaging and packaging systems, collateral systems, and environmental design. Some of the industries covered have included telecommunications, financial services, food and beverage, travel and entertainment, health and beauty care, pharmaceutical, retail, and sports.

An equal balance of strategic marketing and innovative design is essential. The design process for all programs entails research and analysis, concept, refinement, and implementation.

Bright & Associates

Identity for Wavelengths Salon in Santa Monica, California.

▼

Identity and packaging for Eureka Beer. This beer is brewed at a micro-brewery within the star-patronized restaurant of the same name owned by Chef Wolfgang Puck.

▼►

WAVELENGTHS

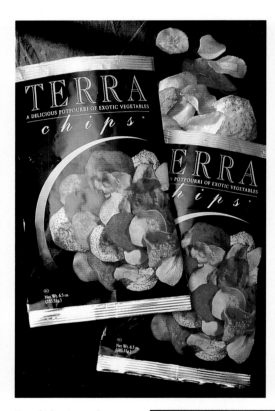

Brand identity and package design for Terra Chips, an innovative snack made from exotic roots.

▲

Brand identity and package design for Ethel M Chocolates.

▲

Identity and application for Kirin's Cipango beer, brewed for the American market. Kirin specified that the label design should have a high-end European look and reflect a theme of exploration.

►

Identity for Fuju Futures,
a commodity broker
based in Tokyo.
▶

Identity for Roland
Music.
▼

Identity for Citrus, a classic California restaurant
based in Los Angeles.
◀▼

Corporate identity
application for Andresen
Typographics shows
geometric and futuristic
shapes in the stationery

while the graphic layout
of the type books
appropriately centers
around heads and bodies.
◀▲

Bright & Associates

Identity for Yonex Canadian and U.S. Badminton Championships.

▼

Identity and packaging for Kaepa shoes. Uniquely, the shoe has a double lace which became a major graphic element along with a color coding system denoting style change.

▼ ▼▼

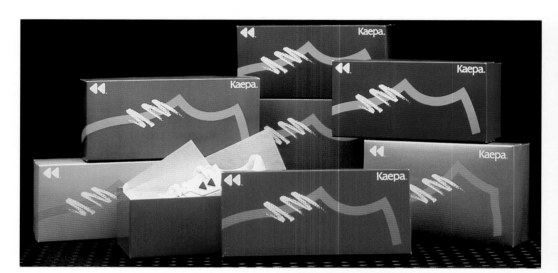

Corporate identity for Aviatecha Airlines of Guatemala. Appealing to both business and tourist passengers, the identity draws from Myan architecture and the colors of Guatamalan textiles.

▲▶

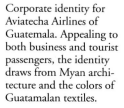

Identity for the Califor-
nia Environmental
Protection Agency.
▼

Identity for Visual Edge.
▼

**Bright &
Associates**

43

Identity program for
National Car Rental, one
of the top rental compa-
nies across the U.S. The
program comprised all
environments, signage,
vehicles, uniforms, and
all print applications.
◄▼

Identity program for
Burlington Express, a
national airfreight and
overnight delivery service.
◄▲

**Bright &
Associates**

Identity for Pinkerton
Security and Investigation
Services.
▼

Identity and application
for the Los Angeles
Sports Council.
▼ ▶

Retail identity applica-
tion for Marauchi
Furniture Access, Japan's
largest furniture store
based ouside Tokyo. The
program comprised an
identity, signage, and all
interior graphics and
vehicles.
▶

Identity and application
for Resort at Squaw
Creek, a $120 million
year-round conference
and resort complex in
Squaw Valley, California.
▲

Identity for CETRA's
(China External Trade
Development Council)
image enhancing
program for Taiwan.
The symbol is awarded
to manufacturers of
excellent products.
▲

Name, identity, and
application for
Mobilworks, a mobile
electronic retailer based
in Southern California.

Identity for Citizen
Forestry Support System.

Identity application for
Western Digital, a
Fortune 300 computer
component corporation.
The new identity conveys
the diversity of products
and services within the
computing field.

▼ ►

Identity and signage
application for
Bullwhackers Casino in
Colorado. Both
Bullwhackers' casinos
were designed as
authentic to the gold
rush era at the end of the
19th century.

▼

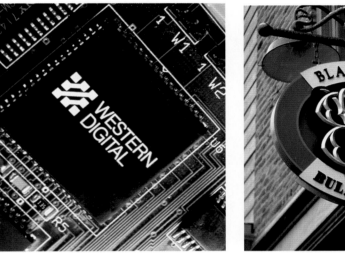

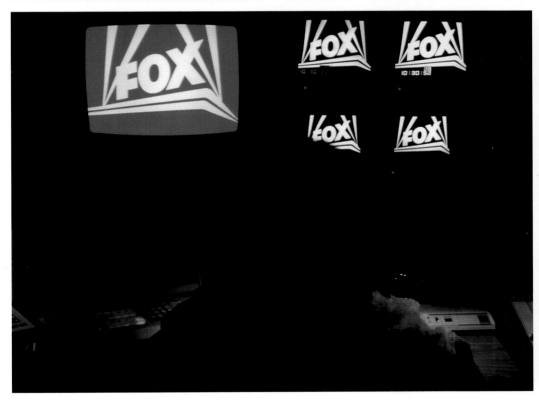

Identity for Fox
Broadcasting. Bright's
intention was to compete
succinctly with the other
lettered networks, but
retain equity and
tradition of search lights
and the name Fox.

Identity and application
for Speedway Cafe, a
stylish restaurant in the
hip area of Venice,
California.

▲

Chermayeff & Geismar Inc.

15 East 26th Street
New York, NY 10010
Tel: 212-532-4499

Principals:
Ivan Chermayeff
Thomas Geismar
John Grady
Steff Geissbuhler

Associates:
Keith Helmetag
Cathy Schaefer

Where once aquariums were simply repositories of fish, they have today developed into highly sophisticated public institutions that encompass related bird and animal life, the earth's water systems, and environmental concerns. Working with its sister company, the architects Cambridge Seven Associates, Chermayeff & Geismar have developed graphic identities for a variety of aquariums around the world. Depending on its location, each aquarium is based on a different water-related concept. The graphic identities reflect those differences.

Alaska SeaLife Center

BALTIMORE AQUARIUM

ACQUARIO DI GENOVA

New England Aquarium

OSAKA AQUARIUM
RING OF FIRE

Tennessee Aquarium

Chermayeff & Geismar Inc.

Chermayeff & Geismar Inc. has developed over 200 graphic identities for a diverse range of clients, including large and small corporations, cultural institutions, government agencies, television networks, stores, hotels, and even national celebrations. Each has presented a special identification problem to be solved. Thus the designs take many forms — symbols, logotypes, acronyms, monograms — and encompass a great variety of styles. But common to each is a shared underlying approach, appropriate to the purposes and needs of the business or institution it represents, and meaningful to the audiences who will see it.

**Chermayeff &
Geismar Inc.**

The objective for this Hispanic–American television network was to create a bold, meaningful, and memorable trademark, especially for on-air use.

The initial letter "T" triggers the word "Telemundo" and also subliminally stands for "Television." The green globe within the "T" stands for "Mundo" (World). The

bold shape of the "T" is suggestive of a window to the world.

For promotional purposes and specific programs, round icons such as balls (soccer, tennis,

baseball), film spools, flowers, sun, moon and balloons, can replace the globe within the "T".

TELEMUNDO

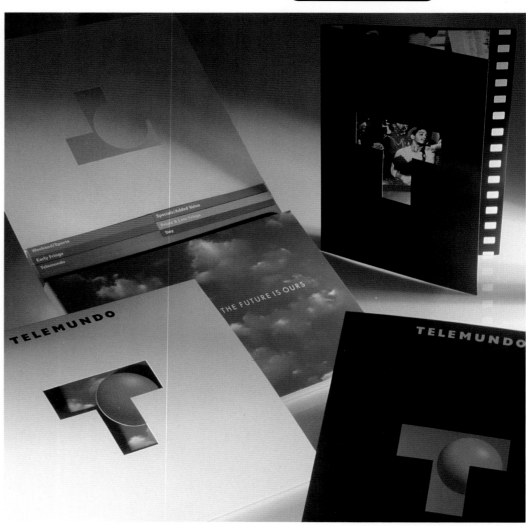

This identification is for Tempozan Marketplace, a major waterfront retail marketplace located in Osaka, Japan.
▼

This identity was created for the Turkish conglomerate Koç and its operating units, the Rahmi M. Koç Collection, the Sadberk Hanim Museum, and Koç University.
▼ ▼

This is the identification for Nissay (Nippon Life Insurance), the world's largest insurance company.
▼

This corporate identification is for Tokio Marine, a major international property insurance company based in Tokyo, Japan.
▶

Chermayeff & Geismar Inc.

Ordinarily the starting point of a corporate identity project is a new symbol or logotype; however, the decision was made to retain the existing logotype which had considerable recognition. Now renamed "The Knoll Group" after its purchase by Westing-house and subsequent merger with three other furniture companies, it was in fact a different company, with its own business goals. An updated visual identity was created to better meet these new goals and to unite the four brands under a single identity.

The design program builds on the modernist tradition so long associated with Knoll, but does it in new, fresh ways, featuring bold use of the logo and colorful overlapping imagery.

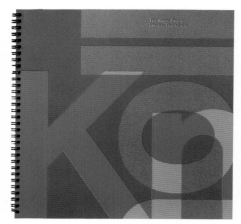

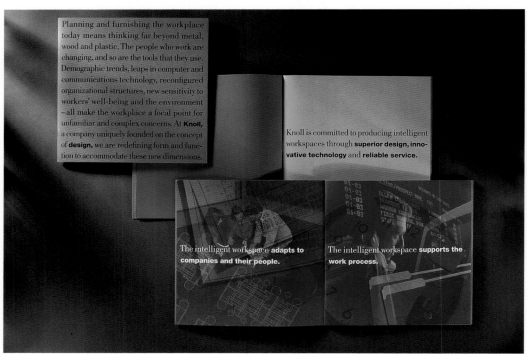

Gemini Consulting was formed by the merger of two U.S.-based management consulting firms and is one of the fastest-growing such firms in the world.

Seeking to set Gemini apart from its competition, nearly all of whom have names derived from the founder's family, Chermayeff & Geismar developed the name and

then conceived a simple, memorable word mark. The image derives from the Gemini legend of bright twin stars that, in Roman times, guided sailors on their voyages. The stars, replacing the

dots over the letter "i's", are eccentrically positioned to suggest forward movement.

GEMINI

Chermayeff & Geismar Inc.

The Business Paper Division of Crane & Co., manufacturers of only the highest quality 100% cotton fiber papers, had no consistent identity and was using a wide variety of visual forms for the Crane name. To make the business and specifier community more aware of the Crane brand, a contemporary trademark and graphic look was created. The symbol, a combination of the letter "C" and the Crane bird, identifies the division and gives it a distinct personality. The decorative qualities of the symbol allow it to be used as an illustrative device on covers, packaging, folders, and other promotional material.

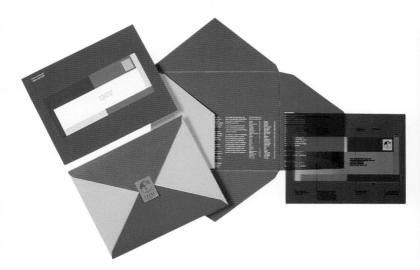

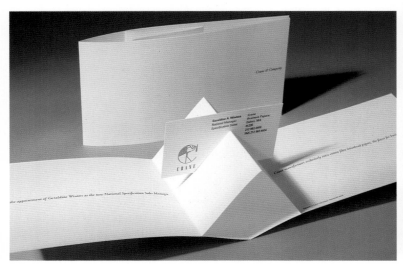

Crafts organizations throughout North and South America designated 1993 "The Year of American Craft." Using an image of hands as a symbol of craftsmanship, the mark is used in the appropriate local language.

▼

This is the identity for Merck & Co. Inc., a research-intensive manufacturer of human and animal health products and specialty chemicals and for its international division MSD (Merck Sharp & Dohme).

▶

Below is the corporate identification for Conrad Hotels, the international subsidiary of Hilton USA and its international hotels.

▼ ▼

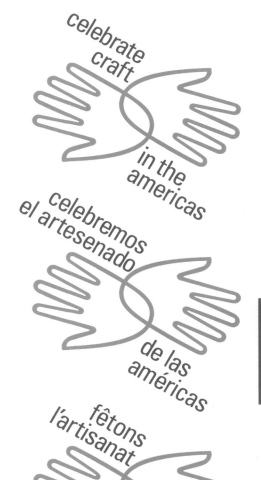

54

Coley Porter Bell
4 Flitcroft Street
London WC2H 8DJ
Tel: 44 0 71 379 4355
Fax: 44 0 71 379 5164

Haulmark: The creation of a new name and visual identity for the pan-European rail freight services to operate via the Channel Tunnel. The image and name had to be recognizable with German, French, and English speakers.

▼

Carling Black Label: Coley Porter Bell translated the lager brand's core values into a strong visual essence to be consistently expressed across all forms of communication, and in particular, to compliment the memorable advertising.

▼ ▼

Gooch and Wagstaff: A confident, eyecatching identity for the firm of chartered surveyors and commercial property agents which created consumer awareness in a difficult marketplace. It represented a young, dynamic company, while remaining authoritative and restrained for the business environment.

▼

Every organization has an identity. It is what makes you stand out when all your competitors appear to be offering the same service or product at the same price.

Ultimately, getting it right can be the difference between success and failure.

Coley Porter Bell can help. They are "soft" enough to understand the human issues, yet "hard" enough to talk effective strategy and practical implementation.

By tapping into the firm's creativity, both in terms of thinking and implementation, their clients have an opportunity to take a more objective, fresh look at their own real strengths; and then to work with the designers to shape and build a new confidence in the future.

Coley Porter Bell

Barclaycard: The "spirit" of Barclaycard captured by a new corporate brand and visual management system, strengthened and rationalized its application.
▼

Chase Global Services: For this subsidiary of the Chase Manhattan Bank, Coley Porter Bell developed a new identity and corporate literature system to communicate their position as market leaders in 24-hour global custody management.
▼

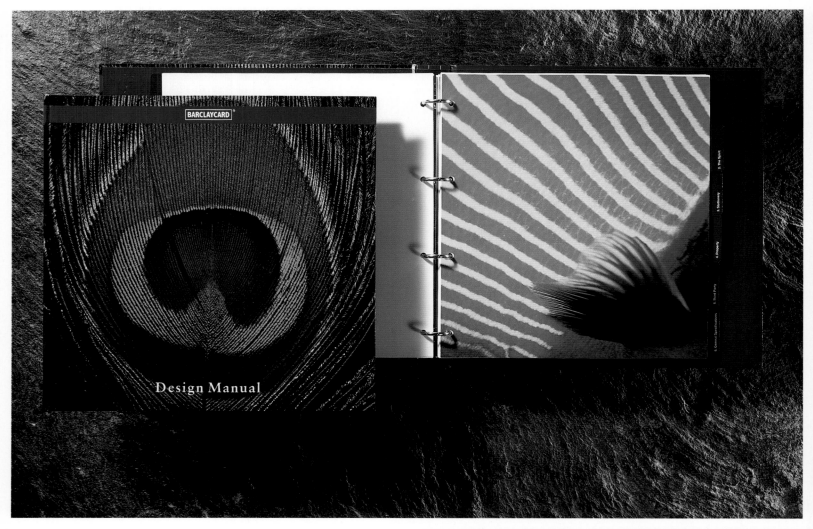

British Red Cross: A campaign identity built on the power of the International Red Cross symbol, to create greater impact in a charity-fatigued market.

▼

CIPFA: The identity repositioned CIPFA, The Chartered Institute of Public Finance and Accountancy, along with the creation of an integrated marketing and communications plan to relaunch the institute.

►

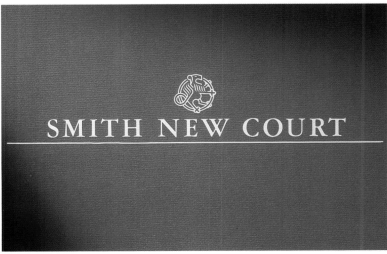

Smith New Court: This leading stockbroker's firm operates worldwide from four geographical bases. Coley Porter Bell implemented a color-coded system to differentiate the geographic regions, build up a structure, and set presentation style standards in order to achieve global recognition and communicate a unified corporate message.

◄

Scottish Pride: The merger of two companies resulted in the relaunch of Scottish Pride. The new visual identity was developed alongside revolutionary corporate branding design.

▲

University of North London: A full communications strategy allowed the development of a corporate identity program to focus on the positive values of the University. The visual identity was applied to all stationery, literature, signage, and the University building.
▼

BSM: Adopting the new Vauxhall Corsa for training purposes gave BSM, The British School of Motoring, an opportunity to strengthen its corporate identity through livery, retail outlets, and the famous 'pyramid,' as the world's largest driver tuition organization.
▼ ▼

Master Choice: The repositioning of its label range for A&P, the fourth largest food retailer in the U.S. The corporate brand and packaging was developed to establish a strong unique element of the stores' appeal.

Coley Porter Bell

Mills and Boon: The creation of a structured corporate design system for consumer books and guidelines for style and cover illustration.

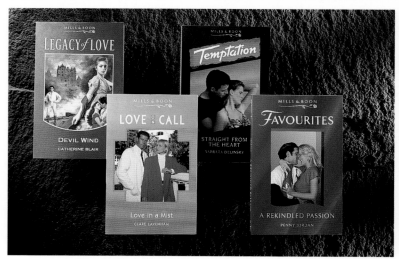

Bloomsbury and Islington Health Authority: The merger of two health authorities combined two very different cultures. The newly developed identity evoked the common theme of "care"— a value that was equally motivating to both organizations.

▶

BLOOMSBURY ♡ ISLINGTON
HEALTH AUTHORITY

Typhoon: A repositioning for the sportswear manufacturer to maintain its reputation for high-quality equipment; but also to attract the young, fashion-conscious growth market. The new identity has established the basis for a capital investment programme and the development of new markets.

◀

NPI: The competitive repositioning of NPI in the pensions market and new visual identity created by Coley Porter Bell maximized the established values of NPI and redefined the company for its new business-to-consumer environment.

▲

Desgrippes Cato Gobé Group

18 bis, avenue de la Motte-Piquet – 75007 Paris
Tel: (1) 45 50 34 45
Fax: (1) 45 51 96 60

New York
411 Lafayette Street
New York, NY 10003
Tel: (212) 979-8900
Fax: (212) 979-1401

London
Park Place
Lawn Lane, Vauxhall
London, SW8 1UD
Tel: (71) 582-5151
Fax: (71) 582-5160

Tokyo
2-25-18 Minamimagome
Ota-Ku, Tokyo 143
Tel: (03) 3778-1729
Fax: (03) 3778-1957

DESGRIPPES CATO GOBÉ GROUP

INTERNATIONAL GROUP FOR COMMUNICATION BY DESIGN

In 1992 the challenge for Ann Taylor was reconsideration by the marketplace. Although the chain was still a strong competitor, it needed to reclaim its lost customers and attract new ones. The design objective was not to drastically transform the image of Ann Taylor but to revive and capitalize on its brand equity and develop a vehicle that would carry the store into the '90s. The positioning defined for the brand personality focused on the values of authenticity, balance, emotion, and relationships. The design objective was to capture these values and to suggest a connection with the customer. The packaging, natural color, and texture of the paper evokes authenticity and in keeping with '90s values, all the packaging is made from recycled materials and is recyclable.

Personal details were brought out through elements such as the shapes of the boxes, the way the ribbon wraps the boxes, and the photograph of a friendly woman on the small shopping bag. ▼

The first feminine perfume line created for Boucheron was inspired by the ring of the famous jeweler. After this worldwide success, came the Boucheron masculine perfume line. Harmony between the men's and women's perfume universes was achieved through the gold and blue colors and the famous godron's design. ◀

Desgrippes Cato Gobé Group

Unique among the world's top design networks, Desgrippes Cato Gobé Group is a private, independent partnership of individually well-known design companies firmly established in their respective markets located in the world design centers of Paris, New York, London, and Tokyo. The group, with a staff of over 140 marketing and design professionals, achieved a turnover of $21 million in 1992.

The group is composed of teams of creative and marketing professionals, specializing in strategic imaging (SENSE), corporate identity programs, product development, packaging, retail, signage systems, audiovisual design, print, and other communication supports.

The synergy of talents and experiences of each of the offices allows for a creative and strategic response to all communication by design problems encountered in the various national and international markets. The Group is enriched by the sharing and exchanging of each team's expertise. While the offices remain independent in their national markets, they pool their talents for European and international projects. This original structure offers the Desgrippes Cato Gobé Group a unique view over innovative techniques and social and cultural developments around the world. This structure is the base for their observational research tecnique: SENSE.

They believe that the unique combination of strategic innovation, creative excellence and effective, computerized implementation provides winning design solutions for their clients.

Desgrippes Cato Gobé Group

For the Italian fashion brand Genny, Desgrippes Cato Gobé created the corporate identity, the feminine perfume line, and a line of bath products: elegant and sophisticated, modern and timeless, without mannerism.

▼

When Desgrippes Cato Gobé created the young woman's perfume line for the Italian fashion brand Byblos, their inspiration came from the images of music and history that this name evokes: the antique Byblos, city of dreams, between desert and sea. The object that holds the perfume had to recreate the miracle of light and infinity which Nature framed in the ancient city: the various blues of the sky and sea and the ochres of the desert. The bottles take the form of Amphoras with which the ships were laden when sailing from Byblos. The leitmotiv for the entire line is that pearl of the desert, "the desert rose." Stylized, it becomes the brand's logo and appears in gold on the bottle.

▲

The challenge was to retain the value equity that has always been part of the Thom McAn brand while bringing back a sense of fashion. Desgrippes Cato Gobé achieved this goal without sacrificing the high-quality message "Spirited Living," which was chosen to define Thom McAn's brand personality and reflect an approach to life which is expressive, upbeat, and confident.

▶

With the creation of a new feminine perfume line for Vie Privée, Desgrippes Cato Gobé realized that this natural beauty product brand name needed to appeal to today's woman in a new way. The body of the inkstand-like bottle of frosted jade-green glass holds the key to this woman's secret. The case,

with its ribbon and yellow label, takes its inspiration from the binding of a personal diary. The flower-shaped stopper symbolizes the fragrance.

Desgrippes Cato Gobé created a new corporate identity for Sonia Rykiel, as well as newly shaped packaging for the make-up and skin care line, Night and Day. Pos and Beauty Space was also created for a department store in Tokyo.

The cosmetics group Orlane has been a client of Desgrippes Cato Gobé for more than five years. The agency created its new corporate identity and has since worked continually on the design of all its products, as well as its product environment, to create harmonious, modern, and prestigious communication. For the present make-up range "Les Extraordinaires," the agency developed product and package design as well as POP material. The B21 skin-care line blends luxurious sophistication with high technology.

▲

Desgrippes Cato Gobé Group

Technical and sophisticated, Desgrippes Cato Gobé developed the brand identity for the first line of toiletries, skin-care, and eau de toilette for men signed by Gillette. The brand goes beyond the traditional "universe of shaving" and satisfies mens' "every morning" need. The package design was developed after a world-wide study of men's behavior and expectations concerning this type of product. The line is composed of perfume products, shaving cream, stick and spray deodorants, and after shave.

▼

When the well-known Campbell Grocery Group commissioned an innovative new can, they charged Desgrippes Cato Gobé to create an independent brand of pasta sauce for the UK market. In a market where glass packaging is perceived as inherently more upscale than metal cans, the goal was to create an image that was authentically Italian. Utilizing the extensive international image management experience available within the Group, the agency developed the brand personality and name, as well as the graphic design. Overcoming the optical illusion obstacles presented by the can design, they created a natural, wholesome, and yet sophisticated feel for Cianto, bringing to life the full, timeless flavor of classic Mediterranean regional cooking. Combining product photography, original illustrations, the packaging utilizes an Italian green and red color scheme combined with rich accents in metallic gold and is embellished with an original crest. Originally marketed in two varieties — "Traditional" and "Onion and Garlic" — the Cianto personality has already proved so successful that Campbell is developing three new varieties for a future launch. Cianto won both the Gold Award in the processed food division, and the Supreme Gold for best of show in the 1992 Best in Metal Awards from the Metal Packaging Manufacturers Association.

▶

Searle needed to reposition its sugar replacement product. Canderel, which had only been sold in pharmacies. The success of the Canderel line, sustained by the strong and dynamic image of t/he colored sun (designed by Desgrippes Cato Gobé) allowed the company to launch products under this identity: Can'kao, a line of cho-colates rich in cocoa content but low in calories. The packaging of the chocolate bars and the instant cocoa powder entices those with a sweet tooth.

The project strategy was to communicate quality, freshness, pride, and value. The Great American Victory Markets' identity was to embody the "sea to shining sea" values and communicate a family feel, one which invites consumer confidence and loyalty. Desgrippes Cato Gobé strategic design created the new logo which represents those values: red communicates the silo of a traditional American farm. The woodblock style reflects a personal touch and sends a uniquely American message, "this is your neighborhood store which is ready to service your needs." This program entailed a new corporate identity system and translated that system through signage, in-store presence and all its packaging.

For this new yoghurt developed by Chambourcy according to a Greek recipe, we created a design inspired by the mystique and sensuality of Greece. The packaging was the only medium of communication for this product and undoubtedly contributed to its commercial success. In the meantime several range extensions were developed.

Desgrippes Cato Gobé Group

The organizing committee for the Winter Olympic Games of Albertville in 1992 asked Desgrippes Cato Gobé to optimize the logotype of the games and to create a book of standards. A "chart of style" for all possible applications was created: vehicles, decorations of the competitions, and signage systems. The agency created corporate identities and print designs of brochures for the Club Coubertin, Jeunesse du Monde, Parcours de la Flamme Olympique, Equipe 92, and the Olympic Arts Festival. They also created different editions of the Games' Magazine, regulations manuals for all sports, the official poster of the games, and posters for different sporting events.

Desgrippes Cato Gobé created a new corporate identity, architecture, and interior and exterior signage for the Société Générale Marocâine de Banques, one of the most important banks in Morocco. A book of standards for corporate identity and architecture was designed as well as applications in stationery, checkbooks, bank cards, and promotional objects. The agency created all elements for the internal and external launch (video, brochures, invitations, pins) and organization of the corporate identity presentation ceremony, which took place on December 8th, 1991 in Casablanca, Morocco.

▼

Desgrippes Cato Gobé created the corporate identity for the Japanese Educational Group Rissho which included stationery, signage, and a book of graphic standards.

▼

Desgrippes Cato Gobé created the new corporate identity of the SNCF (French Railways). The new symbol was adapted to the evolution of this public service company and reflects its values and ambitions, a strong symbol, it unites all the activities, divisions, and regions of the SNCF.

▲

Founded in 1967 by André Malraux, the Orchestre de Paris is committed to playing a major role in the French and international musical world. The objectives of the agency were to define a new concept of communication, to reposition the corporate identity, and to create the overall stationery applications.

They conceived a new structure for all printed matter, particularly reconsidering the style of media action for the launch of the season and the promotion of concerts.

◄

Part of an overall initiative to improve consumer perception of British Gas, the design developed by Desgrippes Cato Gobé was employed as an important communication tool. A collection of new brochures on various services provided by British Gas was created and included showers, barbecues, and central heating, etc. Although within the British Gas corporate style, particular attention was paid to high-quality photographic styling.

◄◄

For Tag Heuer, Desgrippes Cato Gobé created a sophisticated brochure presenting the high-quality products of this brand of Swiss watches.

◄

DeSola Group, Inc.
477 Madison Avenue
New York, NY 10022
Phone: 212-832-4770
Fax: 212-371-2135

United Artists Theatres
Industry leader,
limited brand equity
– that was the challenge
in creating a brand image
for United Artists
Theatres which competes
in a historically "generic"
business. A business
where customer action
had been driven by the
product, not the theatre.

United Artists Theatres is
the largest exhibitor of
major motion pictures.
Technical advancements
in film exhibition and
expansion of the "cus-
tomer experience" allow
for a competitive point of
differentiation.

These developments
combined with a valuable
heritage creates the foundation for building the
brand. A communica-
tions program that takes
advantage of all exposure
opportunities from the
large screen to concession
packaging provides recog-
nition and awareness.

With its superior multi-
plex design, innovative
promotion programs and
sophisticated purchase
and payment systems,
United Artists Theatres is
certain to be the "Theatre
of Choice."

▶

"Schema"
Michael Netter

D eSola Group assists institutional, unit and product/service management in the broad areas of research and analysis, strategic planning, communications and design, information systems development and implementation management.

The firm works with U.S.-and internationally-based clients in the financial services, retail, industrial, consumer products and public sectors. While consulting principally with Fortune 500 and major financial companies, the firm also contributes to the success of emerging businesses and new products.

DeSola Group emphasizes:
- a contextual view of management needs to support strategic change
- creative, zero-based thinking to assure the most germane perspective
- dedicated, multi-disciplined project teams to encourage program continuity and integrity

The firm's Management and Marketing Consulting Group is most commonly engaged to 1) evaluate markets, 2) align business resources, and 3) structure management processes and supporting technology systems to facilitate superior performance.

The firm's Communications/Design Group develops programs that mobilize and positively differentiate companies and brands within highly competitive markets.

Working as a team, DeSola Group assists clients in realizing success as shown in the examples that follow.

Chemical Banking Corporation
The financial services industry competes in a changing marketplace: customers are becoming more sophisticated, competition is becoming more intense and institutions are able to provide a more comprehensive portfolio. The merger of Chemical Bank and Manufacturers Hanover Corporations responds to the opportunities this marketplace provides. This new "greater" organization will better fulfill market needs and more efficiently manage its business systems.

With the creation of a "new" Chemical, a new "image" had to be developed and communicated. Given the competitive strengths and synergy of the two institutions — worldwide, an identification system that properly communicates the "merger of equals" and maximizes their equity was constructed.

To assure market-responsiveness, an analysis of markets and their needs was conducted. The identification system was then expanded to the organization's business units and to the product level, covering all media opportunities through this highly orchestrated identity system.

▶

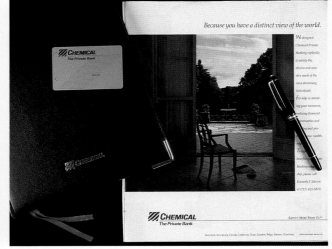

CHEMICAL
The Global Bank

CHEMICAL
The Business Bank

CHEMICAL
The Private Bank

CHEMICAL
The Consumer Bank

CHEMICAL
Geoserve ®

DeSola Group

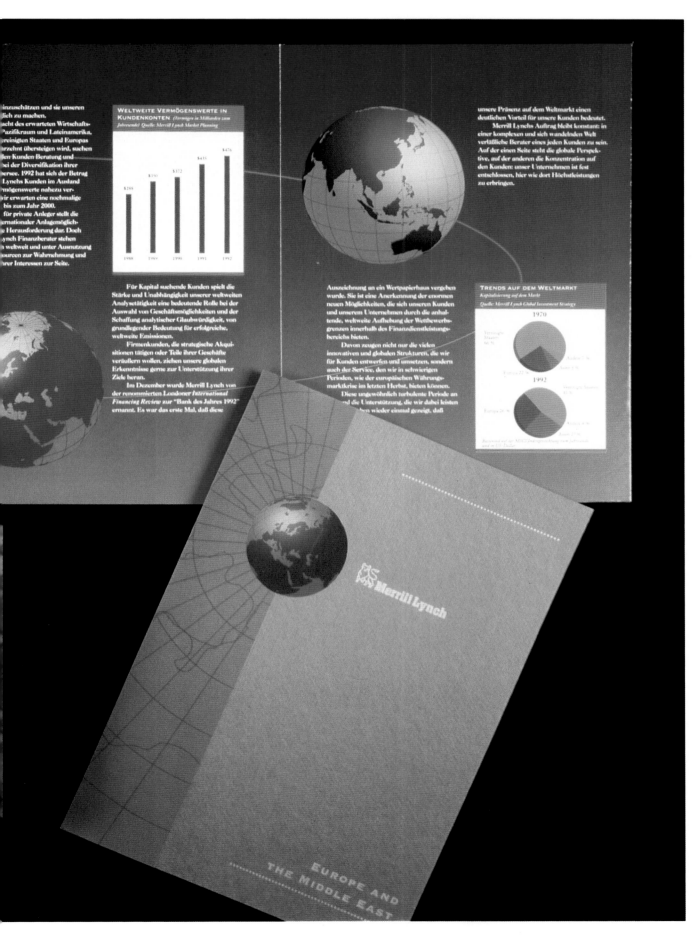

Merrill Lynch

"Merrill Lynch is singularly positioned and strategically committed to global leadership as the pre-eminent financial management and advisory company" — Merrill Lynch positioning statement.

Merrill Lynch has achieved a market position unmatched in the financial industry. It has become a true "mega-brand" of financial services. Epitomizing global servicing, the institution leverages its resources on behalf of its clients to not only access domestic and international markets, but provide superior market intelligence.

To convey the institution's unique capabilities, a complete communications program that leverages the Merrill Lynch identity and communicates the breadth and dedication of the organization was developed and embraced — worldwide.

◀

Dr. Scholl's
Dominant in the footcare category, Dr. Scholl's offers a complete line of products and, based on positive consumer research, is introducing a series of premium products as part of a brand restage. Primary objectives of the restage are to combat private label incursions, provide a more progressive brand image, simplify the sales process, provide added-value to the premium products and jump-start stagnant category sales.

To achieve these objectives, a brand positioning and image strategy was developed that would strengthen the franchise while attracting qualified non-users to the category. Specific recommendations included reinforcing the brand equity, increasing and proving product functionality, expanding the brand meaning to be more relevant to today's lifestyles, and energizing the brand image.

Executionally, DeSola Group focused on product nomenclature, graphic and structural packaging and merchandising systems. Embracement by the trade and enthusiastic consumer response has reinforced the brand's commitment to the category.

▶

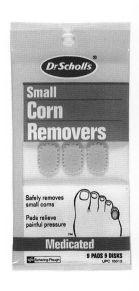

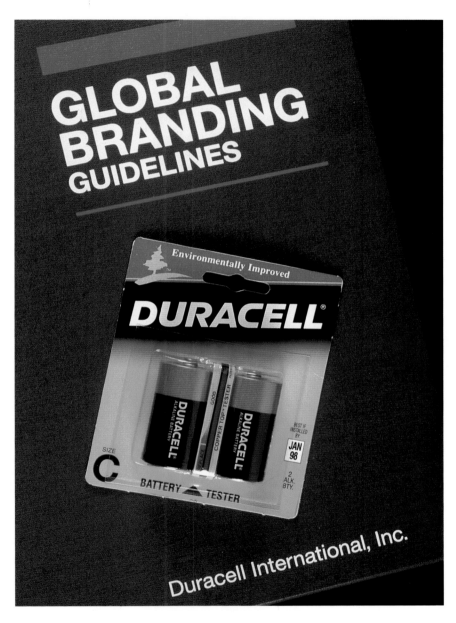

Duracell

"Around the world — in every store." Duracell is the world's leading brand of high-performance alkaline batteries. Recognized as the "source of portable, clean power," it was imperative that the high level of perceived value of the Duracell brand be maintained with current franchises as market presence expands and product development continues.

To reinforce its valuable brand image, DeSola Group developed a series of global branding guidelines to enhance Duracell brand equity as the company continues to respond to domestic and international market opportunities for its core business and beyond.

These strategies and the marketing and communications efforts they direct, further establish Duracell as the best brand of batteries.

Gad Shaanan Design

4480 Cote de Liesse
Suite 390
Montreal, Quebec
Canada H4N 2R1
Tel: 514-735-9550
Fax: 514-735-3961

Comair/Delta Connection, actual interior and concept rendering (shown below).

 ◄

Market analysis
Industrial design
Transportation design
Packaging design
Graphic design
Product engineering
Prototype labs

Enlight Corporation,
Taiwan, snap together
computer casing.
▲

Gad Shaanan Design is an international design consultancy founded in 1980 for clients in a variety of industries, including tranportation, consumer electronics, and industrial products. The company has four divisions to meet all design needs: industrial design, engineering, transportation, and graphic design.

The company, with clients in North America, Europe, and Taiwan, is headquartered in Montreal, Canada, providing clients with a full turn key package from market analysis to product developement, product engineering, drop test evaluation, and packaging design.

Gad Shaanan
Design

Industrial Design

Special Expertise:
Ergonomics and anthro-
pometrics, product
designs ensuring efficient
manufacturing, design to
simplify assembly, pro-
vide production and
technical drawings, in-
house engineering, in-
house model shop.

Partial Client List:

IBM Canada
Bombardier Inc.
Via Rail
General Electric
Acco
Canplas Industries Ltd.
Electrovert Ltd.
Gandalf Data Limited
Ideal Security

Larcan Communications
Inc., UHF/HDTV
enclosure.

▲

Types of Projects:

Portable computers, retail telephones, cellular telephones, automatic teller machines, modular console for 911 emergency services, wave soldering equipment, white goods, compact kitchens, 13G military seating, sporting goods, office furniture systems, on- board equipment for trains, pedal boats.

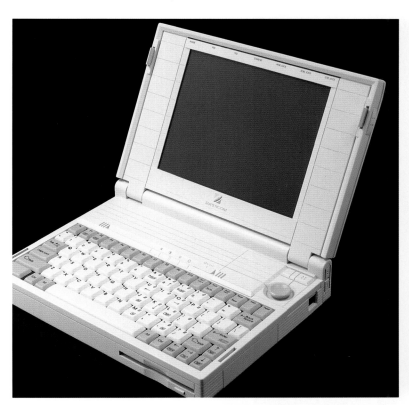

Supercom/Supertron 14" Monochrome Monitor.

▲

Supercom/Supertron 386 Notebook Computer.

Gad Shaanan
Design

Northern Telecom
Canada Inc., JAZZ tele-
phone for the North
American market.
▼

Fuller Tool Co. Ltd.,
Dial-A-Bit Screwdriver.
▼

Northern Telecom
Canada Inc., caller ID.
▶

Graphic Design

Special Expertise:
In-house knowledge for
consumer product pack-
aging, development of
marketing strategies,
development of multi-
lingual packaging, ergo-
nomic graphic develop-
ment on consumer and
industrial products (ease
of understanding, clarity
of the message on the
product for end user),
exterior graphics on vehicles in the transportation
industry.

Partial client list:

AVS Technologies
Fuller Tool
Comair
Visiniti
Hagen
Northern Telecom
Gandalf
Miller Properties
Supercom, Taiwan
Canplas

Supercom/Supertron,
new name and OVA
Corporate Identity.

▼

Opti Caset & Visiniti,
Visiniti Logo Develop-
ment, packaging, cloth
cleaner-P.O.P. display.

◄

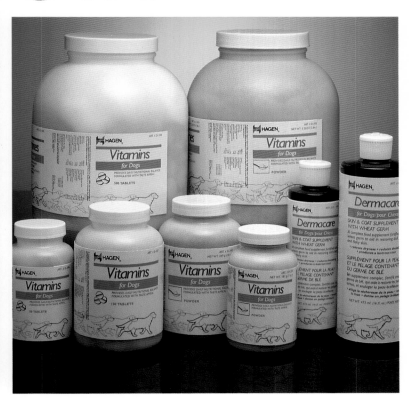

Rolph C. Hagen Inc.,
Vitamin Packaging.

▲

**Gad Shaanan
Design**

AVS Technologies Inc.,
Nikko product line,
telephone packaging.
▼

AVS Technologies Inc.,
Nikko product line,
audio & video packaging.
▼ ▼

AVS Technologies Inc.,
Nikko product line,
CD and personal stereo
packaging.
▼

AVS Technologies Inc.,
Nikko product line,
headset packaging.
▼ ▼

Transportation Design

Special expertise and types of projects: Cabin layout, seating design, galley design, lavatory design, architectural development and lighting, full range of design consultancy services to clients, design capability for all types of commercial, and commuter aircraft, experienced with on board services, specialize in exterior graphic applications, space study mockups.

Partial client list:

Canadair/Regional Jet
Bombadier/
  Mass Transit Division
Via Rail
Lufthansa City Line/
  Germany
Comair

Bombardier/Canadair Aerospace Group, interior concept rendering.

Via Rail Canada Inc., Seat, table, tray, and chinaware.

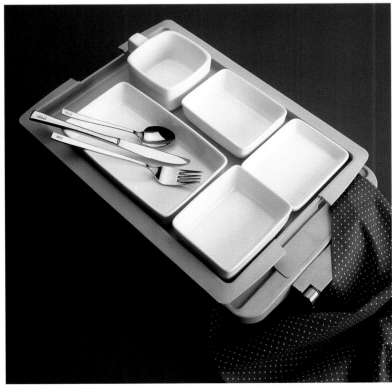

Hartmann & Mehler Designers GMBH

Corneliusstrasse 8
60325 Frankfurt am Main
Tel: 069-756192-0
Fax: 069-746419

The differently designed trademarks and signets of Steigenberger Hotels AG (Germany/Austria/ Switzerland/Spain/ Netherlands/France) lend individuality to the single hotels within the Steigenberger concern. The trademarks reflect the individuality and characteristics of each hotel.

Steigenberger Avance Hotels (Germany/Austria/Switzerland), partner of Avance Hotels, comprises excellent hotels with a relaxed atmosphere in which every guest can breathe more easily and find an oasis in the stress of our world.

Avance Hotels are a living experience in which space has human dimensions and a natural design, and light and shadow are skillfully interwoven. They are a fresh perspective on our workaday routine and discover the world anew.

The attachment of the name "Steigenberger" achieves and reinforces the competence of a sophisticated hotel category to the Avance Hotels.

Hartmann & Mehler Designers GmbH specialize in the development of design strategies for corporate and brand identity, corporate communication, and product and packaging design.

They believe design is a program — an integral part of the respective product or corporate policy — both of which have to be based on an overall, uniform concept.

Complex design programs can only be implemented successfully if a broad range of experience is at hand to provide the foundation for the interrelated areas of brand identity and corporate identity. Therefore, a well-thought-out concept and their step-by-step approach — based on sound marketing knowledge — ensures that the design process is always subject to controls and kept in line with the overall product profile. Hartmann & Mehler Designers' "high-end" computer design stations reduce mechanical work, allowing them to put more emphasis on the creative element of the firm's services.

**Hartmann &
Mehler Designers**

The idea of the new Asbach CI takes into account that the main turnover product, Asbach Uralt, of Asbach GmbH & Co. Rüdesheim am Rhein (Germany), is one of the most traditional trademarks in Germany and as well has a world-wide reputation.

The evolutionary development of the regular product trademark combined with the redesigned word trademark "Asbach" illustrates the new image of this renowned company.

 ▼ ▶

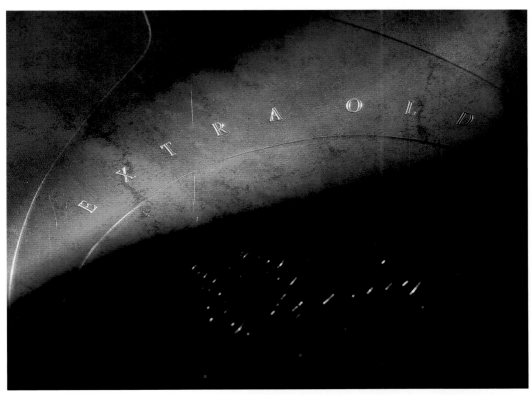

**Hartmann &
Mehler Designers**

The new design development of the Mineralbrunnen AG logo for Mineralbrunnen Überkingen-Teinach AG Bad Überkingen (Germany) contains elements from the previous trademark

such as the star rhombus combined with the new elements of the regional heraldic.

This striking combination injects vigor while reinforcing the tradition

and quality associated with the Mineralbrunnen AG.

▼ ▶

Hartmann &
Mehler Designers

The main criterion for the corporate identity and corporate design of Robert Bosch GmbH Stuttgart (Germany) was to establish a worldwide uniformity for this electronic concern.

The combination of colors together with the style of typography has such broad appeal that the complete trademark also appears in Arabic, Cyrillic, and Japanese.
▼ ▶

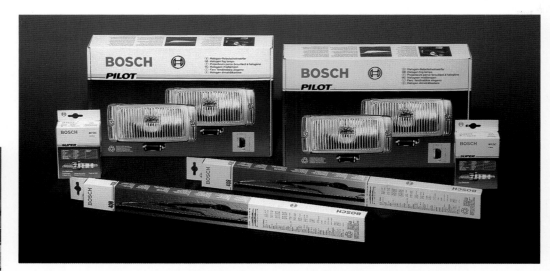

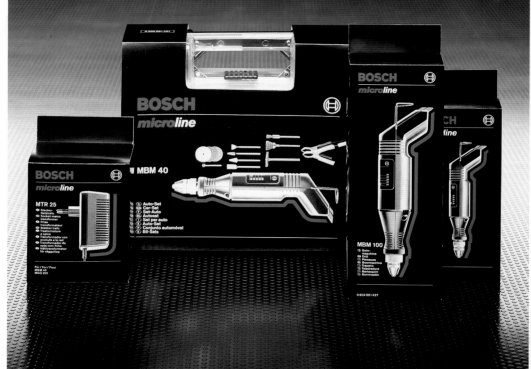

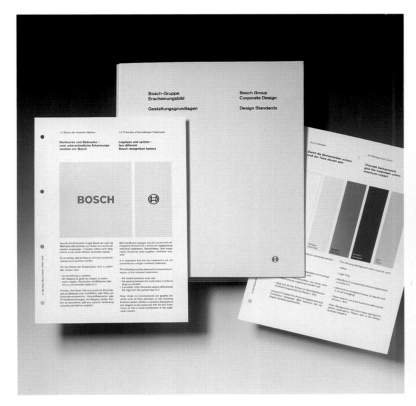

Landor Associates

Landor Building
1001 Front Street
San Francisco, CA 94111
415-955-1400

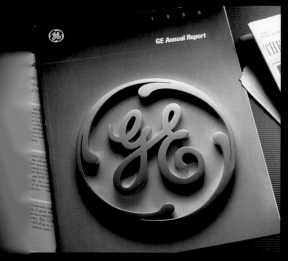

"To sustain our business-es in today's tough com-mercial environment, we must leverage every com-petitive advantage we own. We can't afford for our identity to be misun-derstood; we can't allow our leadership brands to go unacknowledged. As a result of Landor's analy-sis, the direction of change was clear; our identity had to commu-nicate the reality that GE is diverse, reliable and dynamic.

The GE brand, as former chairman Owen D. Young once said, 'may be our least tangible yet most valuable asset. '"

—Robert Costello, Manager, Corporate Marketing Communications, General Electric Corporation

"The challenge was enor-mous: a true trans-national merger of equals with the ambitious objec-tive of integrating to cre-ate a truly new and better company. We needed an identity which could pro-ject the new values of SmithKline Beecham - international, healthcare, innovative, market responsive, technology driven. We were, of course, attracted by Landor's global capabili-ties. More impressive was a sense of over-whelming client commit-ment and a single-mind-ed focus on the job. I know Landor more than did their part from the initial research interviews

It was all done in record time, with Landor giving us on-time performance, quality results and com-mitted professional peo-ple - and we had fun doing it!"

—Henry Wendt, Chairman, SmithKline Beecham

"Landor Associates has helped a long list of the world's leading corpora-tions plan and develop corporate and brand identity programmes. This experience was brought to the fore in solving complex and wide-ranging problems encountered in the devel-opment of the new visual identity for NEC. The full strength of the Landor group has been utilized in this process with three offices - Tokyo, San Francisco and London - making partic-ularly important contri-butions to the project. The positive results achieved give testimony to the creativity, interna-tionalism, and advanced

technology that have been applied. Through its many contributions to the successful develop-ment of the new NEC corporate identity, Landor has shown why it has won a reputation for creative power."

—Yoshihiro Suzuki, Senior Vice President, NEC

Landor
Identity Consultants and Designers Worldwide

THE BENEFITS OF BEING FIRST

In this era of intense competition and marginal advantage, it remains the fundamental value of identity – whether brand or corporate – that makes one product or company preferable to another. But only with astute management, bold creativity and a healthy respect for the consumer will it remain this way.

For over fifty years, clients around the world have come to Landor Associates to assess, establish, reassert or renew their leadership positions within their industries and marketplaces.

Landor Associates' mission in every assignment, and with every client, is to utilize its unique skills in consulting, research, naming and design to build the present and future value of corporate brands.

For years the ferryboat Klamath was their corporate home. It became their symbol and their brand. As Landor earned its reputation as one of the world's creative leaders, it came to signify something even more. Today, the Klamath endures as an icon of innovation.

They have always thought of themselves as pathmakers, and their clients consistently benefit from their commitment to innovation.

Today, their global network of offices is equipped to share a world of marketing knowledge and execute multinational design solutions instanta-

In corporate identity, the benefits of being first are many.

**Landor
Associates**

TOUCHSTONE

Recognizing the demographic implications of the Disney franchise, Landor developed the new Touchstone name and identity to appeal to more mature audiences.

▶

The Most Valuable Corporate Assets on Earth
They are not objects fashioned out of metal, glass or plastic. They are not buildings made of brick and mortar. They are *brands*. Brands built on experience and trust. The principles of branding are universal across virtually

every commercial venture. In reality, a company is as much a brand as is a packaged product. Landor Associates calls these Corporate Brands. Walter Landor once said, "Products are made in the factory, but brands are created in the mind." And that is what Landor still does today — creates

Concorde photo courtesy of British Airways

British Airways has used its new identity to signal a new vision in the most dramatic turnaround ever seen in the airline industry. Here, Landor graphics are applied to the Concorde, the flagship of British Airways' global airline brand.

▲

Landor developed the corporate brand identity for Alcatel, the first truly Pan-European telecommunications company and one of the largest telecom companies in the world.

▶

brands for companies and for their products. In fact, whether one considers the last fifty years or the past twelve months, no company on earth has helped more clients create or renew more identities than has Landor Associates. Its expertise ranges from corporate branding through consumer product branding, to the branding of retail environments. Whether on the stock market floor or on a supermarket shelf, this is an era of intense competition and marginal advantage. It is often the fundamental value of a corporate brand that makes one company preferable to another.

The legendary Cotton Mark was the first of any commodity product to add value through strategic branding. Landor repositioned all-natural cotton as an earthwise fashion statement.

►

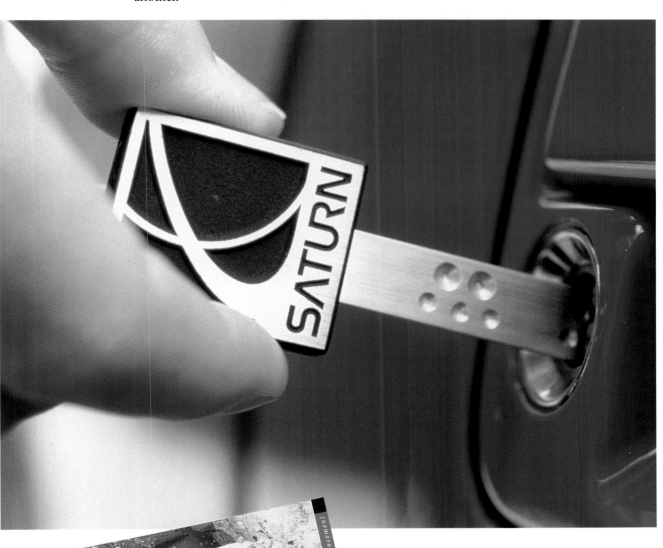

For General Motors' first new automotive division in over 40 years, the Saturn identity was launched, targeted to today's quality conscious car buyer.

◄

Company and brand identity intertwined – Landor created Coke's dual identity packaging system and, for over a decade, has helped Coca-Cola enhance its brands around the world.

◄

**Landor
Associates**

Elegance and sophistication mark the Landor logotype created for Hilton International. This cornerstone of Hilton's new corporate identity is now being applied to its upscale properties around the globe.

◀

INTERNATIONAL

The Art of Renewal
Nothing stands still. The art of renewal is the art of staying ahead. Just a few years ago, most of Landor's business was working with clients to create new corporate and product identities. Today, just as much of Landor's business focuses on ways to give existing identities new life. They call it Brand Renewal. By definition, a *brand* identity worth revitalizing has substantive intrinsic value. Thus, Brand Renewal must seek a sensitive harmony between what is relevant from the past and what will motivate in the

An identity of monumental inherent equity but one in need of organization and enhancement. Through revitalized graphics and consistent visual communication, Landor's identity management program for General Electric has helped GE reassert its position in its many diverse markets.

▲

Landor helped the French oil giant, ELF, invigorate its add-on retail brands and service station environments to compete more aggressively in the Pan-European marketplace.

▶

future. With *corporate* brands, Landor's work is often the consequence of a shift in a company's mission. In these cases, Landor assists its clients in taking advantage of new marketplace opportunities or in helping them communicate a change in long-term business strategy. Each of its clients has separate and distinct needs. But all can benefit from four basic guidelines of Brand Renewal: *Assess* clearly and thoroughly the essence of a company's identity – its underpinnings and equities. *Resolve* the company's future positioning and strategic direction. *Construct* a communications program that builds upon the identity's essence and projects its vision of the future. *Execute* the corporate identity program single-mindedly and decisively.

Landor has created identities for dozens of airlines. This is the dynamic logo for Japan Airlines (JAL), the international carrier rapidly consolidating its position as a world airline brand.

The Hyatt branding system was in need of renewal. Landor's new multi-tiered visual identity updates the image of the hotels and symbolizes the new spirit of the "Hyatt Touch."

Maintaining the equity of DuPont's traditional identity system was the goal as Landor orchestrated the visual communications for DuPont's complex family of companies and products.

Landor's calligraphic solution for Fuji Film's visual identity and the vibrant coloration of its packaging have enabled Fuji to compete head-on in world markets.

Landor
Associates

Landor's identity work for the World Wildlife Federation illustrates the emotional power of graphic symbolism which transcends nationality, language and cultural distinctions.

A World of Difference
Wherever you look in the world today, you will find Landor's work. Landor Associates is worldwide *and* worldwise. Landor has evolved into a truly global company. In a typical year the firm will work on virtually every continent, across dozens of industries, and for hundreds of companies which operate regionally, nationally and internationally. But Landor's uniqueness is not simply a matter of being bigger. Landor has grown to meet the needs of its clients who have grown and expanded into new markets, new products and

Who does not wear Levi's? Landor's original back pocket patch logo still symbolizes the vitality of the world's largest clothing manufacturer.

Landor has created identities for over 100 financial institutions in the past decade alone. Recently, "la Caixa" marked the 10th anniversary of its ground-breaking Landor identity program.

The legendary Dunhill brand had confused its markets. Landor restaged its identity, more clearly defined its target audience, and re-created its retail centers around the world.

new cultures. Any company, from the smallest local enterprise to the world's most ubiquitous product giant, must touch its audience in some particularly appropriate manner. With offices in major cities around the world, Landor provides a local and a regional insight, and a design sensitivity unique in its industry. And by connecting its professional teams together through sophisticated telecommunications, Landor has created the largest and most experienced global corporate identity network in the world. And that, for Landor's clients, makes a world of difference.

A very distinct Landor look for a member of Korea's Kumho family of companies. The whimsical leaping frog for Kumho Delivery Service sets KDS apart from its competition.

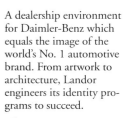

A dealership environment for Daimler-Benz which equals the image of the world's No. 1 automotive brand. From artwork to architecture, Landor engineers its identity programs to succeed.

For the Nobel Foundation, Landor developed a branding strategy for investment and symposia activities as well as an identity system for Nobel Week in Stockholm.

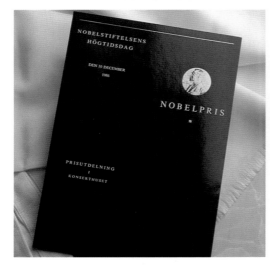

Atlanta to Nagano. Landor identities for both the 1996 and 1998 games represent great creative challenges — creating global "brands" that must look fresh years from now.

Lee Communications, Inc.

11 Conant Valley Road
Pound Ridge, NY 10576
Tel: 914-533-2325

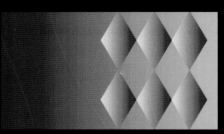

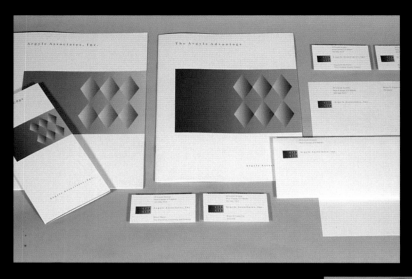

Argyle Associates, Inc. is a management consulting firm specializing in helping its clients achieve high levels of quality technology, product assurance, and process improvement through total quality management. Argyle's identity, which consisted of an outlined argyle graphic and dated typography, was clearly inappropriate for a company considered to be at the forefront of quality technology. Argyle retained Lee Communications to structure a new identity and marketing system that would position the firm as a leader in the quality management field.

The new Argyle graphic created by Lee Communications retains the previous symbol's overall configuration, but recasts it as a three-dimensional element, utilizing two-color gradient tones to achieve a distinctive, high-quality effect. This identification unit serves as the company's main visual identifier, and retains the basic recognition value of the old identity. The new identifier is incorporated into a design system that includes stationery, forms, a capabilities brochure, a marketing folder, and other communications materials.

▲▶

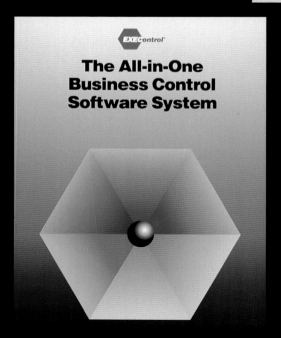

Developed by Ebeling Associates, EXEControl Software for Business is a comprehensive system for managing all areas of a company's business from a single central database. A visual identifier was created for the name EXEControl, together with a design system for marketing materials and user manuals that accompany the company's products.

The hexagon in the visual identifier represents the six vital functions accomplished by the EXEControl system. The bold italic letters, combined with the hexagon in reverse and positive form, project a contemporary, state-of-the-art image.

▲▶

"As a management tool, EXEControl offers the advantages of cutting edge technology."

Lee Communications, Inc.

Key Areas of Expertise

Image Analysis & Planning,
Corporate & Brand Identity,
Name Development,
Corporate Identity Systems,
Standards & Usage Manuals,
Communications Planning,
Design & Editorial Services,
Capability Brochures,
Annual Reports,
Marketing Support Programs,
Package & Product Design,
Exhibits & Displays

Partial List of Clients

American Express,
Argyle Associates,
Blue Cross Blue Shield,
Cambium House,
Copper Development Association,
Darwin Capital Management,
The Equitable,
Essilor of America /Silor,
The Fairchild Corporation,
General Reinsurance,
The Oxford Medical Group,
The Prudential,
Prudential Securities,
Technimetrics,
Tocqueville Asset Management,
Wilmington Trust

L ee Communications, Inc. is an award-winning communications planning and design firm specializing in the creation of strategically designed corporate and brand identity, and communications media. The firm is committed to helping its clients gain competitive advantage through the coordinated utilization of visually compelling design solutions.

Strategic Design Process
• Analysis of needs and opportunities
• Definition of objectives and criteria
• Development of viable creative concepts
• Assessment of candidate solutions
• Refinement and finalization
• Implementation in appropriate media

The Benefits to Clients
Lee Communications' objective-driven planning and creative process has proven beneficial to companies large and small in a wide range of businesses. Strategic design, targeted to corporate and marketing objectives, enables their clients to consistently realize maximum return on their communications investment.

Consultants in Identity,
Communications Planning,
and Strategic Design

11 Conant Valley Road
Pound Ridge, NY 10576
914 533 2325

Offices in New York City,
and Westchester

Bob Lee
President

Lee Communications, Inc.

Lee Communications, Inc.

Copper Development Association

The Copper Development Association Inc. (CDA) is the advanced engineering and market development arm of the copper and brass industry in the United States. The CDA "Trimark," designed in the mid-sixties, has identified the association since its formation.

In 1992, new applications were designed to capitalize on the Trimark's heritage and the recognition it has achieved.

Contemporary sans-serif letterforms are incorporated into the identification system to convey the association's forward-moving programs, as well as to reflect the timelessness of the metals themselves. As part of the CI program, Lee Communications developed stationery, forms, marketing support materials, signage, and other communications media.

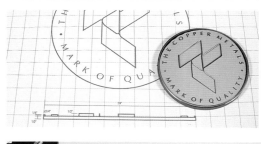

Darwin Capital Management, Inc. is an investment firm specializing in the financial counseling of high net worth individuals. The visual identifier combines classic "chiseled-in-stone" lettering with a five-line, diagonally accented overscore suggesting the layers of information, or investment alternatives, that

Darwin provides its clients. As part of the identity system, Lee Communications developed designs for stationery items, and for client presentations.

Banner Industries, holding company for a variety of manufacturing businesses, needed a new identity following several major acquisitions and divestitures. Having acquired the historically valuable Fairchild name in a prior acquisition, the company adopted its preemptive form, "The Fairchild Corporation" as the company's new corporate title.

The Fairchild visual identifier was created combining bold, custom-designed italic lettering with the three-dimensional, bi-directional "Multimark," to symbolize the company's forward thrust and the interaction of its aerospace businesses. Stationery, forms, signage, and other key communications materials were developed as part of the program.

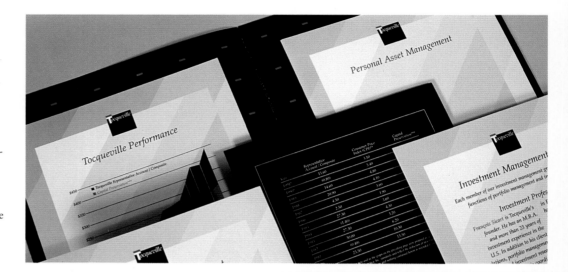

Toqueville Asset Managemant L.P. suffered from an outdated identity featuring an illutration of Alexis de Toqueville, French statesman and political philosopher of the early 19th century. A new CI system was needed to project more appropriately the image of astute asset management and contemporary investment philosophies.

In creating the new identity system for Tocqueville, Lee Communications blended traditional cursive letterforms with a bold sans-serif "T" within a deep blue square, and added a red cursor-like graphic above the T. The resulting identification unit conveys a classic/contemporary quality, along with the stature and solidity that accurately reflect the organization. Stationery, a capabilities brochure, performance charts, biographical sheets, and a presentation folder were created as part of the program.

The Oxford Medical Group's new identity is designed to reinforce its image of a top-quality medical care provider, while conveying the warm caring environment that typifies the Oxford medical centers. Focal point of the new identification system is a large letter "O," in blended tones of yellow and orange, combined with the full name in dropshadowed classic letterforms to form a distinctive, unified identity unit. In stationery applications, the unit appears on a white field with thin lines providing a structure for supporting copy, while in promotional literature, the unit appears on a blended field of orange and yellow with the name in white. The corporate color scheme

reinforces the warmth suggested by the image criteria.

As part of the new identification program, stationery, forms, direct marketing materials, signage, print advertising, and other communications materials were developed.

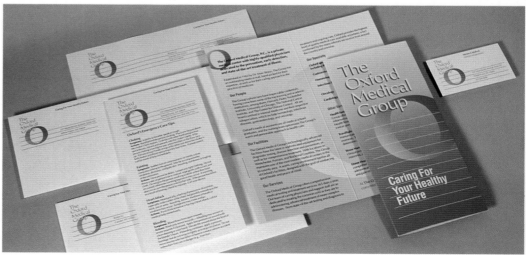

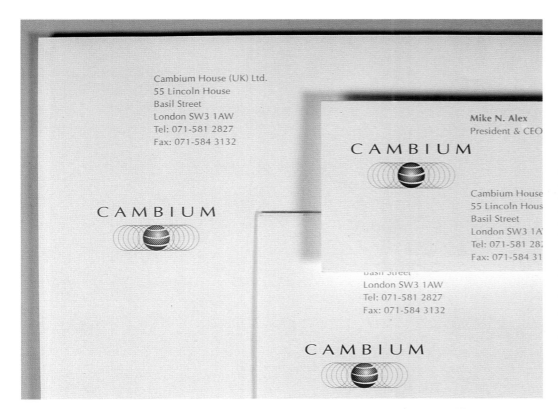

Cambium House Ltd. is a London-based consulting firm providing investment professionals with sophisticated systems, hardware, and related services required to effectively structure, manage, and trade global portfolios.

The visual identifier created by Lee Communications is designed to convey the firm's global scope and its expertise in information exchange systems by symbolizing multiple rings of information radiating from a global core. This high-tech, state-of-the-art graphic is complemented by the classical character of the custom-modified serif letterforms.

The identification program included stationery, forms, and other key applications.

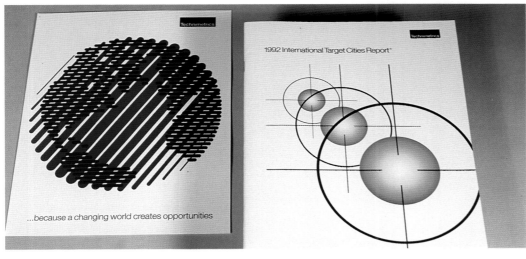

Technimetrics, Inc. is a major provider of accurate databases of financial and executive decision-makers around the world. Founded in 1968, the company image had become fragmented, due in large measure to its straight-type "identifier" and the multitude of disparate designs used in its printed materials. The firm's management recognized the need to develop a distinctive, coordinated identity system ro reaffirm Technimetrics leadership position in its industry.

The Technimetrics identifier was designed using sans-serif letterforms within a rectangular holding shape, projecting the company's stability and strong foundation. Twin diagonal bars projecting as accents over the "i"'s suggest the dynamics of maintaining 100% accuracy in the company's fast-changing database product lines.

A wide variety of communications media, including stationery, forms, a capabilities brochure, sales promotion pieces, packaging, brand marketing materials, and print advertising were developed as part of the program.

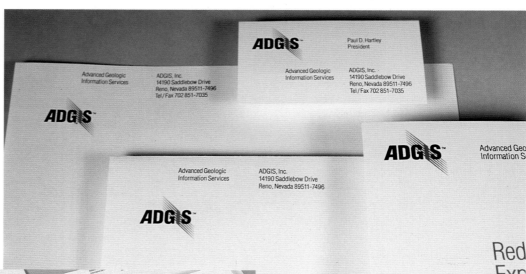

Adgis, Inc. is dedicated to the discovery, evaluation, and development of world-class, low-cost ore deposits through the integration of earth sciences and advanced data processing techniques. Lee Communications developed the Adgis identifier to suggest the firm's stature in its industry, and its expertise in the field of exploration. The laser-like graphic element that forms the letter "i" conveys layers of strata, as well as the multiple datasets used in successful site selection. Integrated with the bold sans-serif letterforms of the rest of the name, this focal element symbolizes the company's high-technology approach to advanced geologic research.

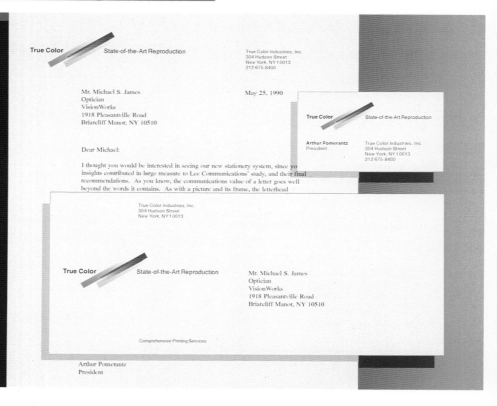

True Color Industries is a New York City printing and graphics organization specializing in high-quality printing at very competitive prices. The visual identifier created by Lee Communications symbolizes the firm's quality and creativity through the use of three over-printing bands of color, representing the three process colors: cyan, magenta, and yellow.

The identification system also included new stationery and customer forms.

DonahueAssociates

Donahue Associates is a personalized employment agency providing permanent placements on a highly selective basis to its corporate clients.

Lee Communications created a visual identifier that suggests the selection process, symbolized by the rising gradient band, culminating with the name Donahue Associates, provider of the process. The communicative name "Donahue" is highlighted in gold.

Lee Communications applied the identifier to designs for stationery and signage.

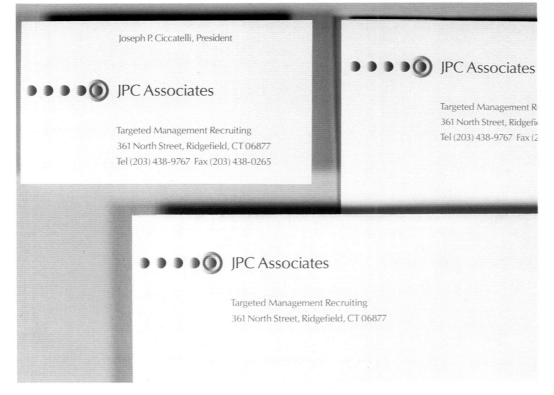

 JPC Associates

JPC Associates is a management recruiting firm that forms close working relationships with client management in order to understand and fulfill their personnel needs on an ongoing basis.

Lee Communications coined the term "Targeted Management Recruiting," and designed a graphic unit symbolizing multiple candidates flowing to a target. This unit is combined with classic letterforms to convey a professional image to the management of the firm's clients.

Lippincott & Margulies

499 Park Avenue
New York, NY 10022
212 832-3000

The St. Paul Companies: Corporate and subsidiary nomenclature and visual identity system to reflect company's long-term goals.
Flagstar: Name and visual system to convey TW Services' mission and leadership in foodservices.
Praxair, Inc.: Identity positioning, new name and visual system for industrial Gases Company spun out of Union Carbide.
Signature Flight Support: New word mark and visual system for Page Avjet to reflect its focus on customer service.

Harcourt General: Corporate wordmark and visual system to help General Cinema gain in recognition for its new business focus on publishing.
Harcourt Brace: Symbol/wordmark for subsidiary of Harcourt General and prototypes for its visual system.
Baskin-Robbins: Image strategy, updated brand design and prototypes for new visual system.
Schuller: Logotype and positioning tag line for Manville Sales Corporation to convey core businesses.

Infiniti: Identity strategy, name, logotype, design concept and comprehensive visual system to launch new auto entry.
CaliforniaMart: Communications analysis, positioning strategy and identity system.
The Gillette Company: Identity positioning and improved symbol to reflect global personal products leader.
Sunoco/Atlantic: Retail identity system, updated logotype, retail graphics, facilities design, signage and nomenclature to reposition offerings.

Lippincott & Margulies

As a leader in the field of corporate identity and image management, Lippincott & Margulies provides comprehensive consulting services to the world's most notable businesses. Their aim is to create a plan of action that will enable their clients to achieve their image goals. In the process, L&M's consultants help formulate those goals and define the unique image attributes that differentiate the firm's clients and their offerings. The firm recommends names, and verbal and visual communications systems, that will help achieve the client's desired image, and then implements the recommendations with teams of expert designers and naming specialists. From Amtrak and Xerox in the firm's early days to The Gillette Company and Samsung today, Lippincott & Margulies continues to develop organization, product and service identities that endure through time and change.

IBM: Development of integrated communications systems based on customer input and identity strategy. System includes packaging, promotional materials, training and sales materials for application development software and office systems. Distinct visual systems add up to a cohesive visual look for three families of IBM software products and services, as well as the organization offering them.

AT&T: Design of new long distance calling/credit card compatible with verbal and visual identity systems previously developed.
Samsung: Visual system including corporate stationery, signage, vehicles and production identification.
Triarc: Name, logo and visual system to link heritage of parent company to its outstanding operating businesses.
Univa: Umbrella identity to represent food product businesses and differentiate holding company from its subsidiaries.

"We were able to work with the end users
to create the optimum design solutions."
*Wayne van Verspoor, Project Manager,
Lippincott & Margulies Inc*

Strategic Direction

Strategy Statement

Continental Airlines

August 2, 1990

Continental Airlines will become a prefe
leisure travellers around the world. Ou
assertive nature as a company, are our

Our success depends on our customer
We will invest to ensure superior pers
they need to achieve the status we se

One recent and challenging project
that required all of Lippincott &
Margulies' services was a
comprehensive identity and image
management program to assist
Continental Airlines in its goal of
becoming a world-class airline.
Continental called on Lippincott
& Margulies to identify the airline's
critical image issues, develop a plan
to resolve them, and implement
the solutions. The first phase of
the program, initiated in February
1990, involved intensive research
among employees, customers and
travel agents to determine the
prevalent perception of the airline.
After a careful assessment of
management's strategic goals,
Lippincott & Margulies' project
team recommended that
Continental adopt a core image
strategy to present the image of a
"world-class, top-quality airline,
consistent and professional in
both its operations and its service,
yet personable, dynamic and
responsive."

Lippincott & Margulies
redesigned all of Continental
Airlines' communications components to reflect the new global
image, from corporate and internal
communications materials to signage, advertising, and marketing
and promotional pieces. The image
management program encompasses
all airport facilities and city ticket
offices, as well as the aircraft fleet
throughout the world.

February 1990				
Strategic Direction	Intensive research among employees, customers and travel agents revealed that while most people believed Continental was changing for the	better, the company's poor service image persisted. Research further suggested that the company's red, orange	and gold colors, red-and-black logo, and other elements of the identity system made it difficult to convey the carrier's new vision.	

"Soft leather seats were fashioned
for the first-class cabin as they
are for the interiors of fine
automobiles." *Constance Birdsall,
Vice President and Design Director,
Lippincott & Margulies Inc*

Interiors

The interiors were
designed with an
understated, relaxed,
uncluttered feel.

Diagnostic Research

Employees
Travel Agents
Customers
Non-customers

...rline of business travellers and frequent
...usiastic, innovative workforce, and our
...etitive advantages.

...riences with and perceptions of our service.
...rvice. Our employees will have the tools

...nternational airline with

Competitive Positioning and Image Goals

Design Criteria and Design Solutions

Proven Results

Research and analysis formed the basis for creating the criteria to rebuild Continental's image as a quality, global airline.

June 1990			August 1990		
...Interiors	**Everything in the cabin was designed to ensure lasting comfort. The aircraft's interior palette consisted of blue and gray hues that were used in a variety**	**of textures and materials. Customers reported they felt more relaxed and comfortable and the airline seemed more professional.**	**Visual Identity**	**Research revealed that a combination of blue, white and gold for the new logo would convey an image of a world-class operation that is stable,**	**dependable, and geared toward the service needs of the frequent business traveler.**

Visual Identity

"The oranges and reds of Continental's old logo were seen as regional and recreational, inappropriate for an international business carrier."
Steve Lawrence, Senior Vice President, Lippincott & Margulies Inc

Among the alternatives tested were variations of the letter "C" and a distinctive globe to convey the idea of "international."

Lippincott & Margulies designers produced various logos in different combinations of blue, white and gold.

Continental

Lippincott & Margulies Inc

"Employees have a stake in the results. They should be included at every key step. And we were."
MD-80 Captain

Uniforms

The uniforms are comfortable, flexible, and allow several options to alternate with tops and vests.

January 1991		January 1991			
Uniforms	Lippincott & Margulies worked with clothing designers from Fashion World to create serious and professional-looking uniforms in navy blue and gold.	**Facilities**	A central component of the Continental identity program was made public in September of 1991, with the opening of a 2,500-square-foot facility prototype at the	Houston Inter-continental Airport in Texas. The airport ticket offices and gate area design is a contin-uation of the aircraft interior in terms of	expressing the Continental identity via color, materials and three-dimensional language of the cabin fixtures.

"The facilities prototype was created as a design laboratory to measure its effectiveness and functionality before wide-scale implementation."
Raymond Poelvoorde, Managing Director, Lippincott & Margulies Inc

The ticket counters, which are made of durable, innovative materials, are more comfortable for agents and are inviting to the customer.

"The [facilities are] a continuation of the aircraft interior in terms of expressing Continental via color, texture and form." *Kathleen Boyd, Product Development Director, Continental Airlines*

An award winning canopy hangs over ticket counters in the new east end terminal at New York's La Guardia airport.

Facilities

Serviceware

Every piece of serviceware is part of an integrated set.

Each set was designed with regard to ergonomics to facilitate use and stackability.

January 1991		February 1991	
Serviceware	Like Continental's logo, the serviceware design was based on the geometry of a globe to convey Continental's new international style.	**Event**	Continental formally introduced its new identity at the Houston Intercontinental Airport in Texas on February 12, 1991.

5,000 Continental employees from around the world were invited to see the unveiling of the aircraft's new exterior at a special event inside an airport hangar against a backdrop of sky and hanging clouds. The introductory event served many purposes: to reaffirm Continental's commitment to its people and customers as reflected through its new identity; to explain the evolution of the old identity to the new; and to provide Continental's management team with a means to express its commitment to customers and employees.

Event

Continental unveiled its new image on February 12, 1991, "symbolizing the progress Continental has made and its goals for the future," according to the official announcement made that day.

Continental Vision

"Creating a provocative poster using metaphors to symbolize world-class, innovation and professionalism was key in expressing Continental's new image to their employees and travel agents." *Richelle J. Huff, Account Director, Design Services, Lippincott & Margulies Inc*

Lippincott & Margulies Inc

To ensure that the developing program stayed close to employee opinions and feelings, the project team devised an ongoing system for soliciting the views and opinions of employees and other important audiences, including pilots, ground crews, flight attendants and ticket agents. These employees made up an "Image Advisory Group" and played a key role in shaping the ultimate execution of the program.

December 1990

Implementation

The new identity, created as a result of more than a year's analysis and research, is being phased in over a four-year period in the form of newly designed aircraft exteriors and interiors, rolling stock, employee uniforms, facilities, serviceware, signage, and systems for product and service branding, as well as compatible corporate, marketing and advertising materials.

All marketing communications were developed to communicate the new image and reinforce the globe symbol.

"Our objective is to distinguish Continental competitively by reinforcing its brand identity with every conceivable exposure, whether it is a simple sign on a hangar or a dedicated setting such as a city ticket office."
*Raymond Poelvoorde,
Managing Director,
Lippincott & Margulies Inc*

Implementation

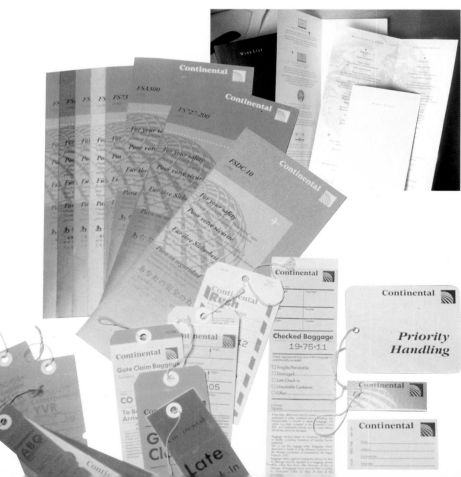

"The day we had the aircraft prototypes secretly flown in for the launch event, air traffic controllers cheered and said, 'Looking good, Continental!'" *Kathleen Boyd, Product Development Director, Continental Airlines*

The final paint selection consisted of blue and gold on a white body, with a three-dimensional globe symbol and a customized typographic system.

January 1991

Aircraft Painting

Three aircraft models were painted as prototypes: an A-300, a 737-400, and a Continental ATR-42 express plane. All paints were hand-mixed and examined in various lights to determine how light would affect the colors at different times of the day. Members of the Lippincott & Margulies design team remained on-site to oversee paint application and make visual adjustments.

Aircraft Painting

Design helped to strengthen Continental's communications by conveying a more professional, international message.

To add excitement to the identity launch event, the aircraft were painted in a hangar in Tennessee, then flown in precisely at the start of the ceremony.

Lipson·Alport·Glass & Associates

666 Fifth Avenue
36th Floor
New York, NY 10103
Tel: 212-541-3946
Fax: 212-541-3947

2349 Victory Parkway
Cincinnati, OH 45206
Tel: 513-961-6225
Fax: 513-281-3611

666 Dundee Road
Northbrook, IL 60062
Tel: 708-291-0500
Fax: 708-291-0516

European Affiliated
Offices:
Brussels
Paris

Left to right: Stevan Lipson, Allan Glass, and Howard Alport.

KRAFT GENERAL FOODS

BATH & BODY
WORKS Brand identity
for extensive line (over
500 SKU'S) of personal
care products for The
Limited's nationwide
retail chain.

NCQHC Identity for
national organization
involved in tracking, ana-
lyzing, and disseminating
information on health
care issues.

STEFANI'S Corporate
and brand identity for
restaurant chain which
also produces product for
retail sales through spe-
cialty stores and food
chains.

KRAFT GENERAL
FOODS Corporate iden-
tity for parent of Kraft
and General Foods.

PROCTER & GAMBLE
Identity update for global
marketer of consumer
products.

Principals:
Stevan Lipson
Howard Alport and
Allan Glass
Year Founded: 1947
Size of Firm
85 Employees
Corporate Identity
Clients Include:
Abbott Laboratories
Baxter International
CAF(Chicago
  Advertising
  Federation)
Coregis
Dean Foods
Dominick's Finer
  Foods
ITT Sheraton
Kraft General Foods
Luigi Stefani, Inc.
Marriott Corporation
Morton International
National Committee
  for Quality Health
  Care
Procter & Gamble
Brand Identity Clients
Include:
E.J. Brach Corp.
Hinckley & Schmitt,
  Inc.
John Labatt Ltd.

Keebler Company
Leaf, Inc.
The Limited
The Pillsbury
  Company
The Quaker Oats
  Company
S.C. Johnson & Son,
  Inc.
USG Corporation
Zenith

Recognized internationally for their work in package design and corporate identity, Lipson•Alport•Glass & Associates (LAGA) is also an important resource for industrial design, nomenclature development, and research. The approach taken by the firm's professional staff is to service the client with unique and creative solutions based on solid marketing principles. Guiding the office's approach to brand and corporate image development is its position that every brand and company has an image that is embodied in the personality and reputation of the organization, product, or service. Identifying the appropriate design attributes (to support the desired image), assembling the appropriate talent for the project team, and involving the client in the process facilitates the creation of solutions that work.

Marriott

A system with three levels of visual and verbal association was established by LAGA to help segment Marriott's different products or businesses. International restaurant chains, in level C, were not required to identify the Marriott association, since marketing and communication benefits were believed to be minimal. For level B the Courtyard lodging chain association with the parent corporation and its global reputation for lodging excellence is a marketing advantage, but Courtyard also has a need for its marketplace image to be dominant. Therefore, for level B the Marriott name and symbol are used as an endorsement. Level A Marriott hotels and resorts position the visual and verbal elements of the parent as dominant communication elements.

The nomenclature and corporate identity for Courtyard and the identity system for Marriott Suites were also developed.

▶

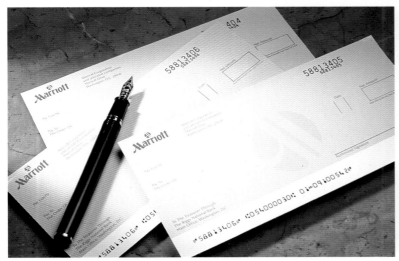

Dominick's image was somewhat fragmented due to a lack of guidelines for packaging, TV, advertising, and vehicles. From development of the wordmark and creation of the packaging system for over 1,200 products, Dominick's identity has been adapted to exterior signs for 100 stores, vehicle fleet graphics, in-store marketing materials, and TV commercials. As a result, the Dominick's name has seen a dramatic increase in awareness.

◀▼

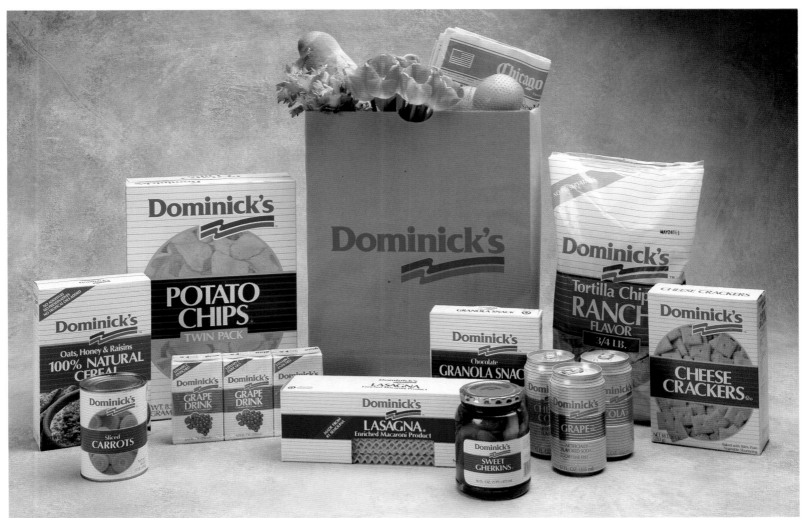

Baxter is an international leader in the distribution and manufacturing of health care products. After acquiring American Hospital Supply Corporation, a 3 plus billion dollar distributor and manufacturer with a strong identity system in place on over 120,000 products and services worldwide, Baxter's management wanted to implement a visually strong Baxter identity that would take the place of the nomenclature and visual style that promoted American to many of the same customers. One of the keys to the company's strength is its sophisticated computer linked distribution and delivery network. The vehicles in the fleet, a visible ingredient of the distribution system, act as rolling billboards for delivering supplies to hospital customers.

▼

Morton International is the parent company of three strong and separate international businesses: industrial and consumer salt products, specialty chemicals, and automotive safety products. Communication inconsistencies with key audiences (employees, plant communities, and financial analysts) existed since the parent corporation, prior to the name change, was Morton-Thiokol. Communications management requested LAGA'S involvement to develop an international identity that would present a consistent image to its key audiences.

▼ ▶

Morton International

126

Lloyd Northover

8 Smart's Place
London WC2B 5LW
United Kingdom
Tel: +44 71 430 1100
Fax: +44 71 430 1490

Branding for Barclaycard, the leading British credit card. Lloyd Northover's identity work for Barclays has included the relaunching of Barclaycard and the identities for Barclays Life, the bank insurance subsidiary, and Barclays de Zoete Wedd investment bank.

▶

Nuclear Electric:
Corporate identity for
British state-owned elec-
tricity generating compa-
ny. The company uses
identity to reinforce its
position as a specialist in
nuclear technology and
to provide a framework
for its public communi-
cations program.
▼

Corporate identity for
aerospace division of
major international
chemical materials com-
pany, Courtaulds.
Courtaulds Aerospace
products are supplied to
aircraft manufacturers
and airlines worldwide.
The business is headquar-
tered in California.
▼ ▼

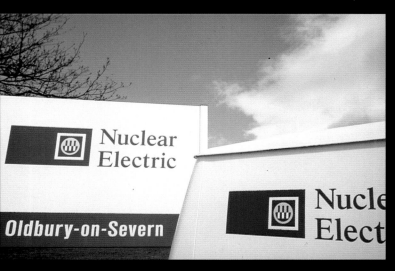

L loyd Northover is a leading international corporate identity, design
and communications consultancy.
The firm helps companies and organizations improve performance by the strategic management of their identity and
communications resources.

They aim to provide a more effective
service through teamwork, strong relationships, rigorous analysis and research,
and exceptional creativity.

The firm's activities include the creation and development of corporate and
brand identities, annual reports, corporate
and marketing literature, as well as the
planning and design of retail outlets,
offices and other business environments.

Lloyd Northover has 18 years' experience working for national and international businesses in all sectors. Based in
central London, the consultancy takes its
name from the two founder–partners,
John Lloyd and Jim Northover, who head
the company today.

Trailfinders: Corporate
identity and interior
design for one of Britain's
most successful travel
companies, specializing
in long distance air travel
packages.
◀

Lloyd Northover

Employment Department Group: Corporate identity for the British Government department responsible for employment and training. As part of the program, Lloyd Northover redesigned the Jobcentres where the unemployed find new work opportunities and sign on for training schemes.

▶

Thames Water: Corporate identity for the Water Quality Centre, a specialist water analysis and consultancy business that is a subsidiary of the London-based water utility company Thames Water.

▶

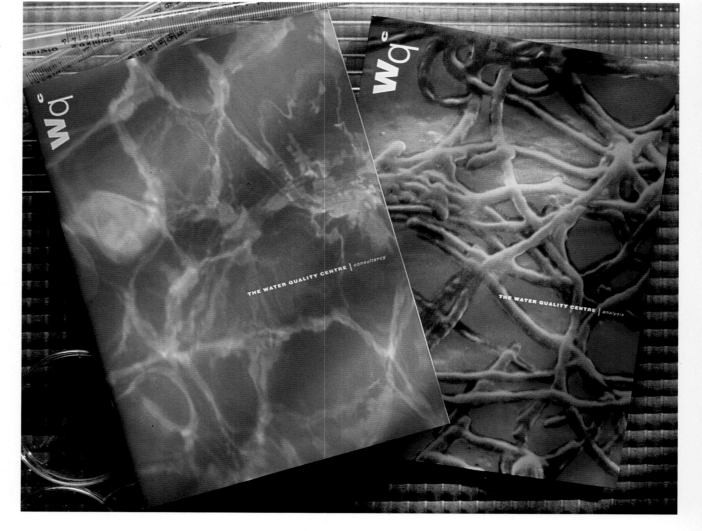

Rockwater: Corporate identity for new under-water engineering company formed by the merger of U.S., British, and Dutch interests. Lloyd Northover created the name and identity to reflect the nature of the business and its environment. The company is now a wholly owned subsidiary of engineers Brown & Root.

▶

BRS: Corporate identity for Britain's market leader in truck rental. The identity program introduced new standards for vehicle fleet marking and all marketing communications.

◀▼

Lloyd Northover

Thomson: Corporate identity for Britain's market leader in tour operations. Updates an earlier version and extends the equity of the Thomson brand. A new identity management system and unified approach to brochure design and marketing communications were part of the program.

▶

Corporate identity for Britain's privatized airport management business. BAA runs the three London airports and those in Scotland. Today BAA is regarded as the world's largest and most successful airport group responsible for the management of airport facilities around the world.

◀

Courtaulds Textiles: Corporate identity for the international clothing and fabrics manufacturer, with facilities in the U.S.A., Europe, and the Far East.

▶

AEA Technology:
Corporate identity for
specialist scientific and
engineering group. The
identity program coordi-
nates the various busi-
nesses and services in a
unifying system.
◄

The Amtico Company:
Corporate identity and
interior design for a leading manufacturer of
high-quality flooring
products. The Amtico
brand identity is carried
through to advertising,
packaging, vehicles, and
showroom design. The
Amtico Company is now
expanding rapidly
throughout the world. In
the U.S., the company
trades as Arteca, under
the same identity.
◄▲

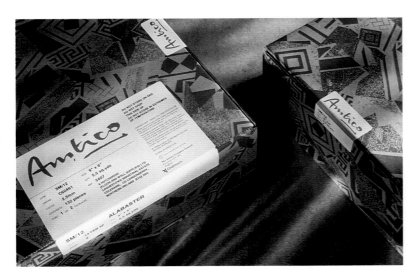

Reuters: Corporate literature reappraisal for Reuters, one of the world leaders in financial and business information. New standards were developed for the Reuters identity in literature to convey the status of the company internationally.

▼

Corporate identity for Scottish Mutual insurance company, helping to position it as a key player in the highly competitive pension, mortgage, and life assurance market.

►

Lloyd Northover

Scottish Mutual

Courtaulds Fibers: Corporate identity for the fibers division of Courtaulds and brand identity for Tencel, the company's newly developed textile fiber manufactured in Alabama.

►

Countryside Commission: Corporate identity for the organization which advises the British Government on country matters in England. The identity has an authoritative tone which differentiates it from the many other organizations in this field.

▶

John Lewis Partnership: Corporate identity for one of the U.K.'s leading department store groups. The identity is designed to reinforce the group's distintive reputation for fairness, quality, and value and to project a coherent image by linking the department stores with the group's supermarket and manufacturing activities.

◀ ▲

Milton Glaser, Inc.
207 East 32nd Street
New York, NY 10016
Tel: 212-889-3161
Fax: 212-213-4072

Campari, LU International and Olivetti each have an illustrious history of using posters as a communication tool. The expressive visual elements of these posters, together with the product name, need no transla- tion and are thus ideal for international audiences.

The LU poster promotes the biscuits with an unex- pected surreal twist to engage the viewer.

The unusual trapezoidal shape of the Campari posters reflects the form of the Campari bottle.
▼ ▶

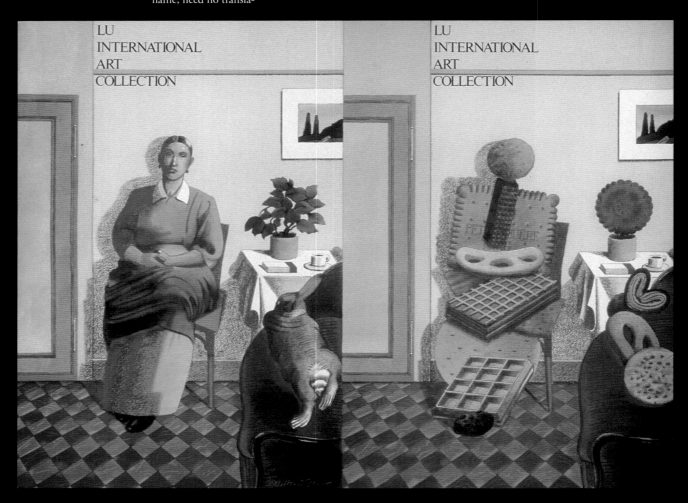

The visual for Olivetti's Praxis electronic type- writer creates an engaging technological image. For the Quaderno, Olivetti's entry into the power book market, we have attempted to create a dis- tinctive and memorable effect by changing the actual shape of the poster to create a three dimen- sional surface.
▶

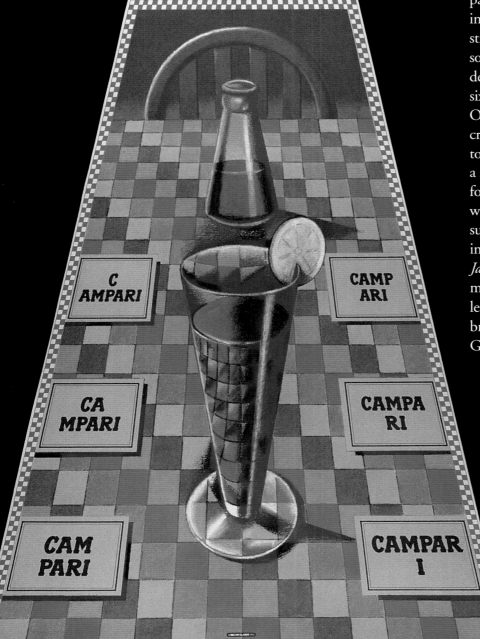

Milton Glaser, Inc. is a multi-disciplinary design firm whose work is celebrated internationally. Their assignments encompass the areas of corporate identity and print and packaging, as well as architectural and interior design. Milton Glaser has had a strong identification with Italy due, in some part, to his years as a Fulbright student in Bologna in the early fifties. In the sixties, he began a relationship with Olivetti, initiated by Giorgio Soavi, the creative director and novelist, that endures to this day. In the seventies he redesigned a number of French publications (several for Jimmy Goldsmith, the same client for whom MGI later redesigned over 200 supermarkets in the United States) including: *Le Figaro, L'Express, Paris Match,* and *Jardin des Modes.* These activities and many one-man shows in European galleries and museums have helped bring a broad international clientele to Milton Glaser, Inc.

Milton Glaser, Inc.

Because of the ubiquitous I (heart) NY logo MGI designed in 1978, the firm is frequently asked to participate in identification or promotion programs for cities. The Barcelona proposals, designed in response to competition, are attempts to create an equally engaging symbol.

▶

The Napoli poster is part of a campaign involving many designers all over the world to restore the cultural image of that city.

▼

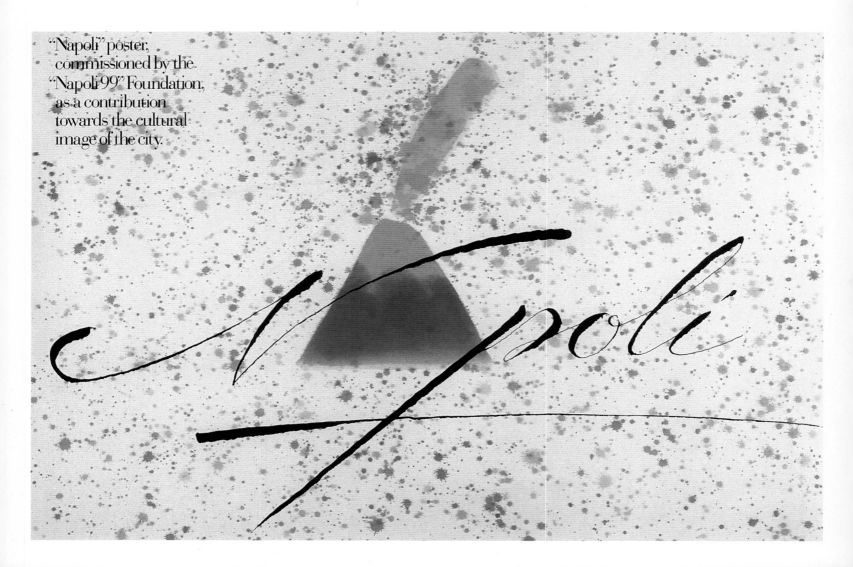

"Napoli" poster, commissioned by the "Napoli 99" Foundation, as a contribution towards the cultural image of the city.

The Seville poster was in response to a competition for the city's world fair in 1992.

Milton Glaser, Inc.

SEVILLA

EXPO 92

The stamps for the United Nations are a recent project in three languages to promote world ecological concerns. They each represent a separate expression of the environment—the personal, the family, the community, the city, the world's water resources, and the earth—universal concerns represented by universally understandable imagery.

Alessi is an innovative and imaginative manufacturer of restaurant ware, pots and pans, tea sets, watches, and a host of other industrial products. In 1988, MGI was asked to create the corporate mark for a new division that would manufacture items in wood. The "twergi," the forest gnomes that were a part of the folk literature of the region, became the name of the division and the basis of the trademark. The only special stipulation was that the design be adaptable to a movable toy (the largest cottage industry of the town is making movable toys, usually cartoon characters). Two projects MGI designed for Twergi are the Aurora table lamp in wood and glass housing a votive light, and a series of cutting boards.

 ▶

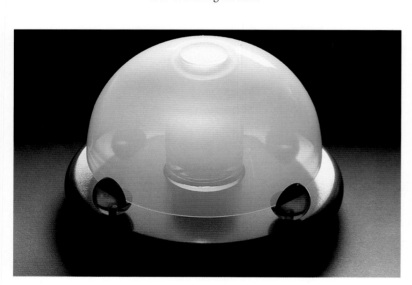

LA CINTURA DI
ORIONE

Con la collaborazione di:
Alain Chapel
Gualtiero Marchesi
Angelo Paracucchi
Raymond Thuilier
e Jean-André Charial
Pierre e Michel Troisgros
Roger Vergé

A cura di Alberto Alessi
e Alberto Gozzi
Longanesi & C.

Storia, tecnica e uso
dei recipienti da cottura
in metallo per
la Grande Cucina

Milton Glaser, Inc.

Founded in 1894, Gundel is the most famous dining establishment in Budapest. Its reputation and physical characteristics had been declining for many years, but new owners George Lang and Ronald Lauder began its renaissance. It has been brilliantly restored and reinvented inch by inch, and has regained its reputation as the finest restaurant in Eastern Europe. The elephant figured largely in the early symbolism for the restaurant (the zoo is next door) and the client wished to continue that theme. The word "Gundel" itself was designed to look as though it was historical, although it is brand new, and forms the basis for most of the corporate communications, as in the two pre-opening posters, (below and facing page) and the menu (with complete listings in English, French, German, Italian, and of course, Hungarian), press kit, and gift certificate (below left). ▼ ▶

142

Nolin Larosée Design Communications

1470 Peel Street
Building A, Suite 700
Montréal, Québec H3A 1T1
Canada
Tel: 514-499-1331

Identification system for Le Mondial de la Publicité Francophone de Montréal, Montréal, Québec. An international advertising competition begun in 1986 and involving the world's French-speaking countries held every other year. The challenge included the development of an identity that was meaningful in the three continents, hence the logotype of the world's first form of advertising, the sandwich man. Applications included trophies, certificates, billboards, and stationery.

1992 Canadian Winter
Games for the physically
disabled

Nadtech Components Inc.

National Council of
Graphic Design Firms

International Centre for
Human Rights and
Democratic
Development

Clockwise, the founders
and associates of Nolin
Larosée Design
Communications:
Clément Larosée, Daniel
Charron, Pierre Nolin,
Marielle Julien.

Founded in 1983, the
firm employs over 20
professionals including
designers, production
and project managers,
and administrative staff.

Nolin Larosée Design Communications

Founding partners Pierre Nolin and Clément Larosée cite corporate identification programs as being by far the most complex and challenging aspect of their successful graphic design business established in Montréal in 1983.

At Nolin Larosée, solutions to corporate identity challenges are developed through a disciplined, realistic approach based on sound business instincts and experience, thorough analysis of a client's market and positioning, an understanding of the business triangle — designer, client and consumer or ultimate client in each project — extensive conceptual research and impeccable implementations. They are business people who speak the same language as their clients. For a client, creating or recreating a visual identity constitutes a major investment in terms of time, energy, emotion, and financial resources. And since it constitutes a corporation's key communication and competitive tool, they believe an identity program is no place to cut your design teeth. Coherent, informed, intelligent, and purposeful design is required.

**Nolin Larosée
Design
Communications**

Corporate identification system for one of Canada's leading trust companies, Montreal Trust, with more than 200 branches and a real estate arm operating across the country. The trust and real estate companies had two distinct images, and the challenge was to create a visual synergy between these two operating units by developing one strong logo for the century-old trust company with subtly different applications for the real estate subsidiary.

MONTREAL TRUST

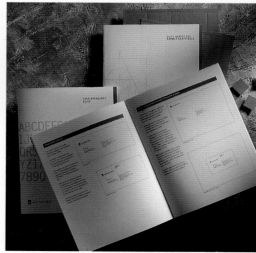

146

**Nolin Larosée
Design
Communications**

Corporate identity system for Laurentienne Générale/Laurentian General. This company resulted from the merger of two century-old insurance companies owned by the Laurentian Group. Nolin Larosée was asked to employ the Group's existing symbol, design a logotype and applications for the new identity, as well as create graphic standards to be subsequently applied to the

Group's various member companies around the world; in essence, the challenge consisted of harmonizing the visual identity of the Laurentian Group's extensive family of member companies.
▼

Identity program for the Town of Repentigny, Québec, which was seeking to ensure its economic development in a very competitive marketplace. The challenge of this particular project was to recreate a visual identity for Repentigny that evolved from its traditional "coat of arms" identification to an image which appropriately reflected its contemporary and dynamic character.

▼

**Nolin Larosée
Design
Communications**

REPENTIGNY

**Nolin Larosée
Design
Communications**

Corporate identity for Telemedia Network, Province of Québec. The challenge was to create a coherent visual identification for Telemedia's six Québec radio stations, including its 75-year-old flagship station, CKAC. The identity had to reflect CKAC's leadership, Telemedia's entire A.M. network, and be adaptable to the various stations' call letters.

Identification program for Fotoclik, Province of Québec. The challenge included the elaboration of a dynamic identity for this new film development company and its more than 50 branches in Québec. The Fotoclik toucan was selected for its brilliant colors, a key factor in film development, and is today a readily recognized logo throughout the province.

**Nolin Larosée
Design
Communications**

SampsonTyrrell

6 Mercer St.
London
WC2H 9QA
Tel: +44 (0) 71 379 7124
Contact: Dave Allen, Managing Director

"A corporate identity consultant has to be able to get under the skin of the client organization, define all of the characteristics by which that organization is recognized and create a workable identity system which identifies and enhances all its communication. This is our business."

Client List
Aer Lingus
BBC World Service TV
British Airways
Cadbury Schweppes
Castrol
Digital Equipment
 Company
Dun & Bradstreet
Electrolux
EMI
Eurotunnel
Financial Times
Hutchison Telecom
Iveco
James Capel
Loctite
Lyonnaise des Eaux
 Dumez

Marks & Spencer
Microsoft
MoDo
National Commercial
 Bank of Saudi Arabia
New York Stock
 Exchange
PowerGen
Price Waterhouse
Royal Mail
ScottishPower
Shell
TSB

Identity issues

Competitive edge	Dave Allen
Global brand or local autonomy?	Professor John Quelch
Privatisation goes public	Terry Tyrrell
Talking business, by design	Peter Widdup
Made in Europe and proud of it	Federica Olivares
The value of identity	Jeremy Myerson
Exploiting sponsorship	Suzanne Bidlake
The power of the brand	Charles Trevail
Check it out!	Josie Bowman and John Slater

Sampson | Tyrrell
Visual Management ™

"In a world where products or services in most business sectors can be imitated virtually overnight by competitors, the need for distinctive positioning and outstanding presentation has never been greater." So says Harvard Business School professor, John Quelch, in his introduction to SampsonTyrrell's latest book, *Identity Issues*. Like the company, the book is a skillful combination of creative excellence and business acumen— a working example of the branded Visual Management™ methodology, which has made its way into the management vocabulary of so many of Sampson Tyrrell's clients.

Formed sixteen years ago, SampsonTyrrell is a leading international corporate identity and design consultancy based in London. The company's sphere of expertise extends from broad-based international corporate identity programs to branding and corporate literature. In 1986, it became part of the WPP Group, the world's largest marketing services group, gaining instant access to the group's extensive international network.

For Castrol, a global brand with a worldwide strategy implemented autonomously at the local level, the traditional approach to identity management is too restrictive. Differences of language, culture and technology from market to market preclude a rigid imposition of rules and regulations. Sampson Tyrrell worked with Castrol to develop a two tiered identity system called "Framework for Imagination," which balances set standards with scope for individual creativity. Together with an ongoing internal communications program, the system has become an important tool for the management of the Castrol brand worldwide.

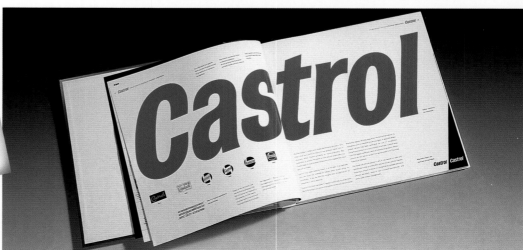

Dun & Bradstreet, the world's largest business information company, needed a revised identity and accompanying external communications program to help them consolidate their market position in Europe. In order to achieve this, SampsonTyrrell recommended the establishment of a European Communications Panel, with representatives from SampsonTyrrell and Dun & Bradstreet. The result of this teamwork is a strong and consistent identity, supported by a whole new level of marketing and internal communications activity.

Digital Equipment Company had an identity in place which had remained untouched for over 35 years. Following a change in management, the visual identity was modified to signal, particularly to employees, the changes which were to take place. At the same time it was crucial that the massive amount of brand equity and commercial value built into the original logo was retained.

SampsonTyrrell worked with EMI to stimulate sales of its British Composers series by creating a family of recordings with a strong identity so visually exciting that previous purchasers re-purchased discs to begin new collections. Sales targets were exceeded by more than 15%.

To maximize Aer Lingus' competitive position on the profitable North Atlantic route between the U.S. and Europe, SampsonTyrrell created a new class of service, Premier, by merging its existing first- and business- class offers. The Premier brand identity communicates to North American and European travellers a subtle combination of visual and physical levels of luxury through minute attention to detailed design of all service elements. The result can be seen clearly in increased market share for Aer Lingus.

▼

As part of the 1990 privatization of Britain's electricity industry, Scottish Power (previously the South of Scotland Electricity Board) had to transform itself into a customer facing, competitive, profit-oriented company. Its resulting new name, new logo and the ways in which these were communicated were developed to embody specific values: technology, quality, power in its broadest sense, and the strengths of being Scottish.

▼▼

ScottishPower

For its sponsorship of Italy's challenger for the 1992 America's Cup, Italian chemicals and materials company, Montedison, launched its own brand, Il Moro di Venezia, to carry its message across the globe. Created not in Italy but in SampsonTyrrell's London offices, the identity had to be applicable not only to the yacht itself, but also to a broad range of promotional merchandise. As well, it had to stand out when reproduced on camera in all kinds of light for all kinds of media.

SampsonTyrrell worked with Mazda to visually upgrade its image throughout Europe, carving out a new European positioning. Design of the dealership network was key to communicating this premium image to the consumer. Mazda's worldwide corporate identity system was tailored for use in Europe, and carried through into showroom interiors that reflect Mazda's customer-focused approach. A simple, supportive framework of guidelines ensured that once the design and consultancy work was completed, Mazda could easily implement the system internally.

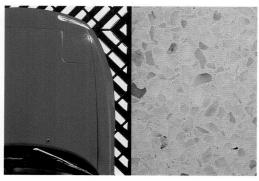

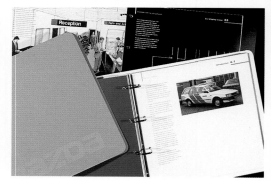

Visual Management makes the documentation and implementation phase of the identity process active not passive. It makes corporate identity a fluid, ongoing exercise, not a book of rules which sits on a shelf and gathers dust. SampsonTyrrell believes in creating ongoing identity management programs for its clients which motivate and energize employees, and result in strong, well-recognized identities.

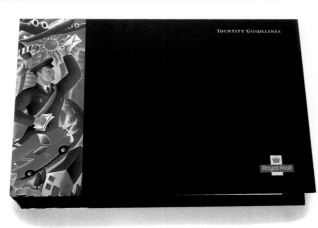

Royal Mail joins Britain to the world and the British to each other. It threads through the community, in business and society, in public and in private. Over the years its technology, function and structure had changed, and it had developed an increasing number of specialized and branded services, all marketed under the Royal Mail banner. It was SampsonTyrrell's task to develop a system to make the Royal Mail corporate identity work effectively across all its various uses, maintaining its integrity, establishing clear visual co-ordination and projecting its overall corporate strengths. It also had to encourage pride of ownership in employees at a time when a new spirit of enterprise and individual accountability was being communicated.

The Schechter Group, Inc.
437 Madison Avenue
New York, NY 10022
Tel: 212-752-4400

LEHMAN BROTHERS

PENNZOIL

NOVON

London Life

Excedrin

The Schechter Group

At a time when a clear sense of direction and sharp customer focus are essential to business survival, multi-national corporations are becoming increasingly diverse and complex. Helping such organizations project their core values and special capabilities to the audiences that determine their success is the business of The Schechter Group. Since 1962, Chairman Alvin H. Schechter and his associates have worked with many of the world's leading business enterprises to better align their permanent communications with their corporate missions. Employing a variety of innovative diagnostic tools, including proprietary *BrandValue*® and *LogoValue*® research, The Schechter Group first clarifies an organization's communications needs and then develops a strategy for satisfying them. The strategy is expressed through a highly focused creative process, in which the development of names and the design of logotypes, packaging, signage, and retail environments may all play supporting roles. The projects described on the following pages demonstrate the firm's creative breadth and its success at providing its clients with what each most desires: a fresh and unique identity perfectly characterizing its culture, which builds on prior equity, while positioning it for the future.

The Schechter Group, Inc.

The marriage between the agricultural businesses of Dow Chemical and Eli Lilly resulted in the world's largest independent agricultural chemical company. The identity challenge posed by this venture required striking an effective balance between the opportunity to leverage the renowned identities of each of the parents, with the need to position the venture as a powerful, stand-alone entity in its own right.

The Schechter Group satisfied this charge by recommending a name that drew on parent equities, rendered in a bold new visual identifier which exemplified the venture's ability to assume a leadership position in the global agricultural market. To achieve this positioning, a dynamic branding model was created and implemented throughout packaging to identify the new company as the source of its cutting-edge chemical and bioengineered products.

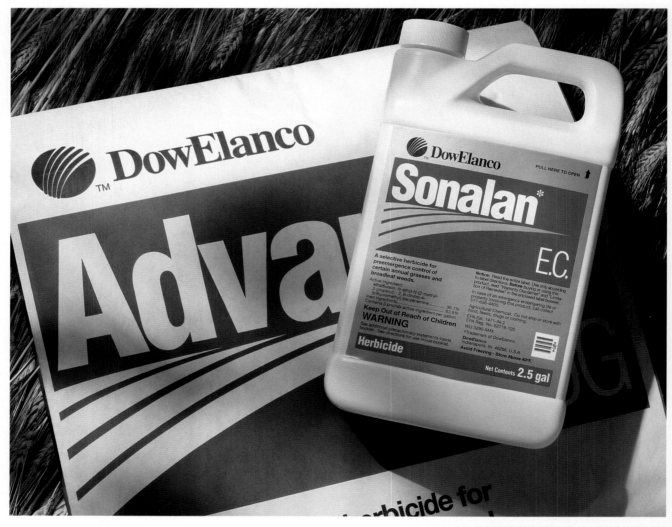

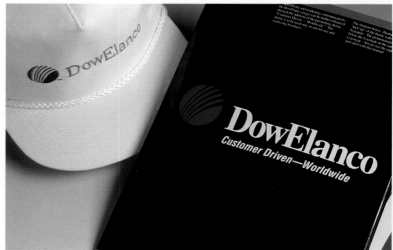

H. J. Heinz Company had an embarrassment of riches. It owned three famous brandmarks—its keystone label with its curving "HEINZ" lettering, the curved pickle, and the "57 Varieties" seal. Yet, none of these famous marks offered the potential to serve as an effective corporate identifier. At a time when man-agement wished to solidi-fy its perception within the global community as a contemporary, broad-based international food processor, this lack of a coherent corporate identity was a significant liability.

▼

Through thorough research and analysis, The Schechter Group determined the need to establish a new Heinz identifier, one which would recast the compa-ny's image from that of a domestic condiments producer. The resulting fresh new look for the Heinz name offered sig-nificant potential to work as a global identifier—leaving the traditional trade dress to operate as the consumer brand on Heinz products, such as ketchup, vinegar, and beans.

Now, some twenty years later, this powerful identi-ty has been a resounding success. It is as contem-porary today as when first introduced and has been instrumental in positioning Heinz as one of the world's leading corporations.

The Schechter Group, Inc.

Kentucky Fried Chicken had reached a watershed. As a brand, it had achieved classic status throughout the world, but the company's growth had slowed as its customers' tastes began to shift to lighter fare. Furthermore, its very name had become an impediment. In an effort to restore a sense of fun and attract a younger, health-conscious consumer, management retained The Schechter Group to help design and orchestrate an image transformation.

Through strategic analysis, The Schechter Group determined that "fried" should be dropped, but the portrait of Colonel Sanders should be retained to assure a seamless transition to reassure the brand's heavy users. Research also confirmed that "KFC" was already used as a nickname by many customers and would gain quick acceptance by all. The resulting identifier was paramount to communicating KFC's transformed image and has served as a powerful brand in international markets.

The George A. Hormel Company had been moving well beyond its core business for more than a decade. Yet its audiences still perceived it to be a meat packer, rather than a broad-scale food marketer. This "all meat" image neither reflected reality nor supported the company's strategic intent to emerge as a major player in food marketing.

The Schechter Group's challenge was two-fold. First, it broadened the image of its flagship brand identity so that it could more effectively address consumers in the grocery aisle. Second, it then communicated Hormel's more diverse corporate identity. The solution included the creation of a new company name, Hormel Foods Corporation, and a new corporate mark. Equally important was an updated separate brandmark which extensive consumer research showed to be more appealing to a broader audience and more appropriate to the whole family eating experience. New packaging graphics were then created to further enhance the uniqueness of individual offerings and to better express what Hormel Foods will be as it enters its second century.

▼

The Schechter Group, Inc.

OSRAM, the pre-eminent German lighting company, wished to expand its presence in North America. Sylvania, targeted for divestiture by GTE, needed a new corporate parent to help fuel its growth. The resulting combination was, in the words of a major customer, "the ideal marriage."

For Schechter, the identity challenge required a sharing of equities. The Sylvania brand would build instantaneous visibility and market position for OSRAM in North America. The OSRAM brand would carry forward a well-earned reputation for innovation and quality throughout the globe.

Schechter's identity solution — a "new" wordmark joining the two names in the distinctive OSRAM Orange. This enabled both brands to benefit from association, and, in the process, revitalized Sylvania and solidified OSRAM's positioning as a global leader.

▼

Visionary chief executives at Sterling Winthrop and Elf Sanofi forged a unique global alliance that catapulted the two entities into the top tier of the pharmaceutical industry.

The partnership of equals presented an unusual identity challenge for The Schechter Group in that management wished to retain elements of their individual logos. The Schechter Group's task involved melding these two disparate designs into a single, cohesive identity for this innovative venture.

The solution — the creation of a symbol depicting a distinctive "soaring bird" — reinforced the new alliance's shared vision, promise, and outlook, serving as a bridge between the Sanofi and Winthrop graphics. This novel solution was further supported by the development of a distinctive identity system, which portrays a unified image across all media, including packaging.

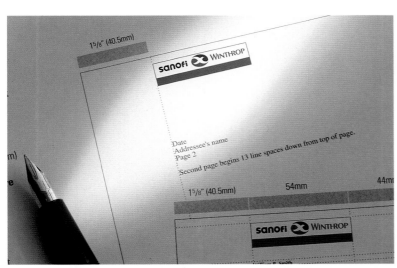

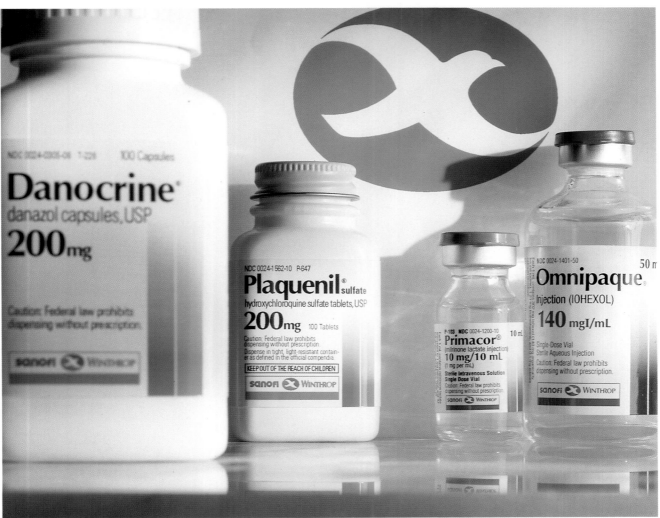

Siegel & Gale

Capabilities

To develop Corporate Voice™ for clients, Siegel & Gale draws on its strengths in strategic positioning, design, advertising, simplified communications, naming, branding, interactive media and, of course, corporate identity.

Locations

New York
Alan Siegel
Chairman and CEO
Kenneth M. Morris
President

Siegel & Gale
1185 Avenue of the Americas
New York, NY 10036
Tel: 212-730-0101
Fax: 212-730-1462

Los Angeles
Siegel & Gale/Cross
Chapman Market
3465 West Sixth Street
Suite 300
Los Angeles, CA 90020
Tel: 213-389-1010
Fax: 213-389-0064

United Kingdom
Siegel & Gale
27 Fitzroy Street
London W1P 5AF
United Kingdom
Tel: 011-44-71-580-0202
Fax: 011-44-71-436-9521

Tokyo
Obun Printing Company
International Network Division
17-2, 1-Chome, Hongo, Bunkyo-ku
Tokyo 113
Japan
Tel: 011-81-3-3817-5930
Fax: 011-81-3-3818-4382

Wellington
Van de Roer Design
11-15 Vivian Street
Wellington
New Zealand
Tel: 011-64-4-3-849-799
Fax: 011-64-4-3-849-776

Toronto
Vandenberg & Co.
54 Berkeley Street
Toronto, Ontario
Canada M5A 2W4
Tel: 416-867-9667
Fax: 416-867-9857

Clients

Acura (Honda)
ADP
Aetna
AlliedSignal
American Medical Association
American Red Cross
AMP
Australian Telecom
Banc One
Bank of America
Barclays
Bell Canada
BP
British Telecom
Capital Holding
Cargill
Carnegie Mellon University
Carolina Power & Light
Caterpillar
Catholic Guardian Society
Chubb
CIGNA
Citicorp/Citibank
Colgate-Palmolive
Crane Business Paper
D&B Software
Dell Computer
DHL
Dow Jones
Du Pont Electronics
Du Pont LYCRA
Ed Tel
European Community Chamber
of Commerce in the United States
Fannie Mae
Federal Express
First Boston
First Interstate
First USA
GE
Girls, Inc.
Gouvernement du Québec
Harley-Davidson
Health-Tex
Historic Hudson Valley
Hoechst Celanese
Honeywell
IBM Canada
IDS Financial Services
Insurance Information Institute
Internal Revenue Service

International Olympic Committee
J.C. Penney
John Deere
J.P. Stevens
Lombard Natwest
McGraw-Hill
Mellon Bank
Metropolitan Transportation Authority
National Semiconductor
National Westminster Bank USA
NationsBank
NBD Bank
New Zealand Trade Board
Northern Telecom Ltd.
Northern Trust
NYNEX
Pac Tel
Paramount Communications
PDVSA
Pitney Bowes
Pizza Hut
PNC
Principal Financial Group
Radio City Music Hall
Roper Starch
Samarec
Scudder, Stevens & Clark
The Boston Consulting Group
The Hearst Corporation
The Prudential
The Rockefeller Group
The St. Paul Companies
The Travelers
3M
Transamerica
U.S. Trust
United Dominion Industries
United Parcel Service
University of California
University of Vermont
USX
Wilmington Trust
World Trade Center
Xerox

Corporations in the 1990s will have to learn to communicate their true substance and character. Not as a fabricated image overlaid on the company, but as an overarching vision, true to who the company is and what it does; one that is integrated seamlessly into all of its communications. Siegel & Gale has developed a holistic approach to communications called Corporate Voice™. It's a far-reaching, practical philosophy that helps a corporation express and manage its personality through every form of communication it employs—from labels to annual reports, advertising to employee newsletters and customer bills. Corporate Voice coordinates all of a corporation's communications, enabling it to speak consistently and purposefully to all of its varied audiences.

The cover of Alan Siegel's upcoming book on corporate voice will feature many in-depth interviews with today's top communications experts and CEOs.

▲

Siegel & Gale recently developed the logo and design program to celebrate the Olympic Centennial. Reserved exclusively for the International Olympic Committee and

▶

worldwide sponsors, the identifier will be used to promote the spirit and enduring values on which the Olympics were founded in 1896.

Siegel & Gale

More than ten years ago, Siegel & Gale created the corporate identification program and graphic standards for the familiar 3M identity. Over time, 3M came to recognize the need for a more complete definition of what the company believed in and stood for in the marketplace. With over 60,000 individual products and hundreds of brands around the world, clarity of purpose and consistency of expression was extremely important.

Siegel & Gale helped 3M and its communications/marketing professionals express the company's distinctive values and personality by developing a concept which bonds the 3M identifier with those characteristics that are most relevant to internal and external audiences alike. Siegel & Gale then created a series of specific booklets which explain in detail how to implement 3M's global identity strategy.

Culture

Values

The 3M Difference

People

Products

Values power the creation of a distinctive Corporate culture

Culture creates an environment that empowers people to pursue their own ideas—encourages individual initiative

Products with innovative attributes and practical applications reinforce Corporate values

People inspired to pursue ideas working cooperatively with customers create useful products

Siegel & Gale demonstrated the unique voice of 3M on employee posters, vehicle markings, and in a spirited employee book. This manual brought core beliefs to life and articulated the philosophy at the heart of 3M's corporate voice.

▶

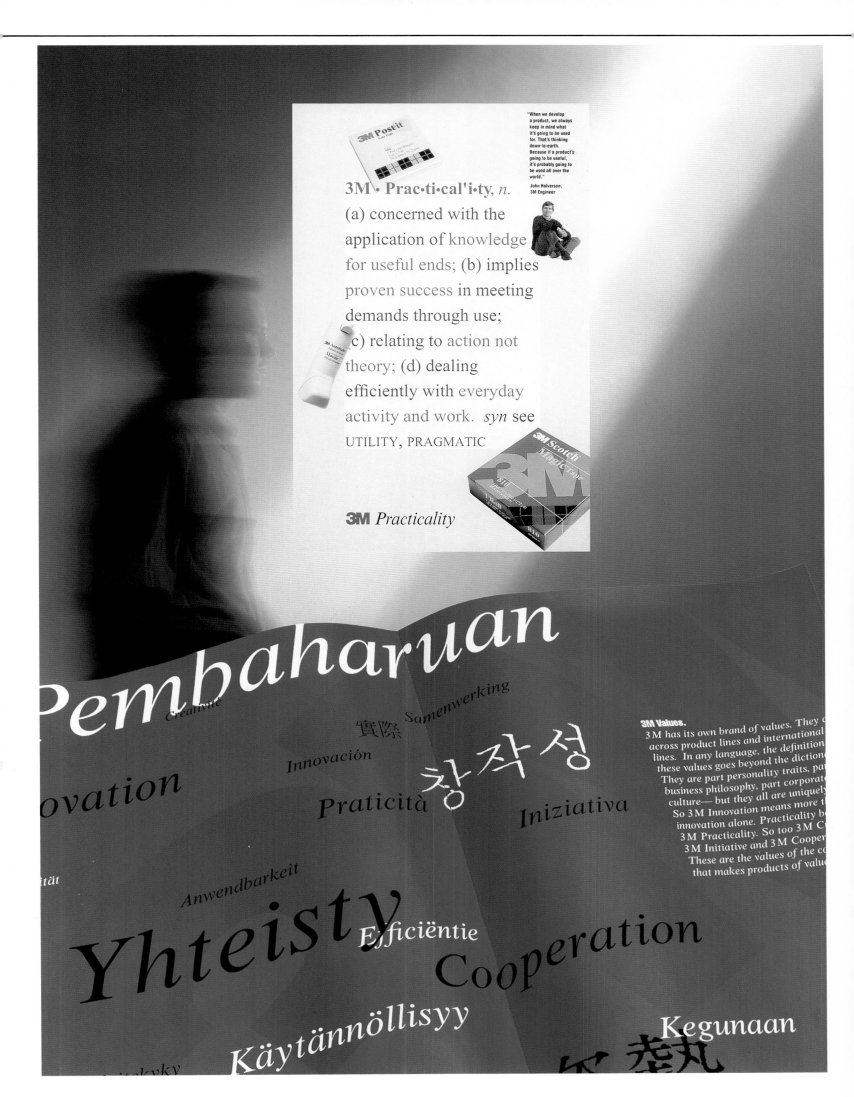

HARLEY-DAVIDSON®
GLOBAL COMMUNICATIONS
GUIDELINES

What the Harley-Davidson brand name represents crosses all social and political boundaries on the globe. To help the people who work for and with the company preserve, protect, and perpetuate the unmistakable sound of Harley-Davidson's corporate voice, Siegel & Gale created a spirited global communications guidebook—translated into the language of every country where the motorcycles are sold. By codifying the mystique of Harley-Davidson, Siegel & Gale was able to help the keepers of the brand—the dealers, licensees, and communicators—maintain the Harley design philosophies in all visual presentations.

Siegel & Gale created corporate voice programs for BankOne, NationsBank, and PNC Bank, among others. The fundamental personality of each financial institution is illuminated by corporate personality statements that are as unique and different as each bank.

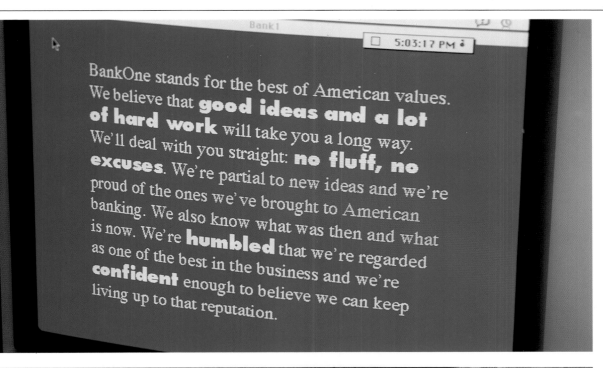

BankOne stands for the best of American values. We believe that **good ideas and a lot of hard work** will take you a long way. We'll deal with you straight: **no fluff, no excuses**. We're partial to new ideas and we're proud of the ones we've brought to American banking. We also know what was then and what is now. We're **humbled** that we're regarded as one of the best in the business and we're **confident** enough to believe we can keep living up to that reputation.

A clear corporate voice expresses a company's personality and position. Even within the same industry, a well-articulated corporate voice will differentiate one company from another.

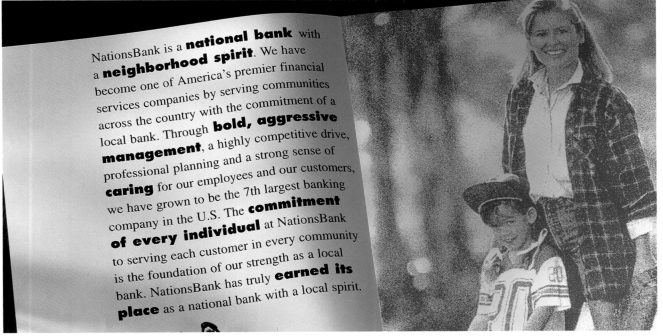

NationsBank is a **national bank** with a **neighborhood spirit**. We have become one of America's premier financial services companies by serving communities across the country with the commitment of a local bank. Through **bold, aggressive management**, a highly competitive drive, professional planning and a strong sense of **caring** for our employees and our customers, we have grown to be the 7th largest banking company in the U.S. The **commitment of every individual** at NationsBank to serving each customer in every community is the foundation of our strength as a local bank. NationsBank has truly **earned its place** as a national bank with a local spirit.

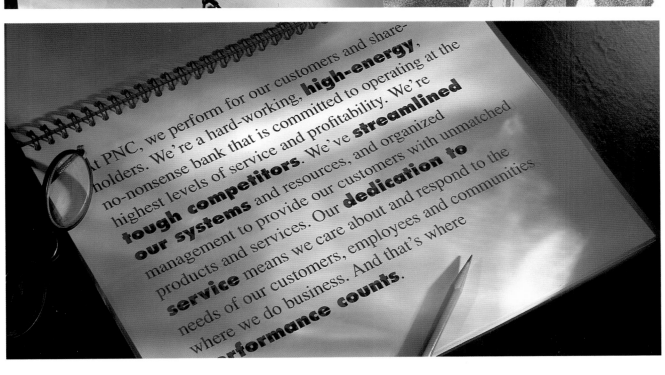

At PNC, we perform for our customers and shareholders. We're a hard-working, **high-energy**, no-nonsense bank that is committed to operating at the highest levels of service and profitability. We're **tough competitors**. We've **streamlined our systems** and resources, and organized management to provide our customers with unmatched products and services. Our **dedication to service** means we care about and respond to the needs of our customers, employees and communities where we do business. And that's where **performance counts**.

D I R E C T O R Y

Addison Design Consultants
575 Sutter Street
San Francisco, California 94102
Tel: 415-956-7575
Fax: 415-433-8641

Anspach Grossman Portugal
711 Third Avenue
New York, NY 10017
Tel: 212-692-9000
Fax: 212-682-8376

B.E.P. Design Group
Rue des Mimosas 44, B-1030
Brussels, Belgium
Tel: 32 2 215 34 00
Fax: 32 2 215 39 11

BrandEquity International
A Division of Selame Associates
2330 Washington Street
Newton, MA 02162
Tel: 617-969-0733
Fax: 617-969-1944
Mdm: 617-332-9076

Bright & Associates
Identity and Design Consultants
901 Abbot Kinney Boulevard
Venice, California 90291
Tel: 310-450-2488
Fax: 310-452-1613

Chermayeff & Geismar Inc.
15 East 26th Street
New York, NY 10010
Tel: 212-532-4499

Coley Porter Bell
4 Flitcroft Street
London WC2H 8DJ
Tel: 44 0 71 379 4355
Fax: 44 0 71 379 5164

Desgrippes Cato Gobé Group
18 bis, avenue de la Motte-Piquet
– 75007 Paris
Tel: (1) 45 50 34 45
Fax: (1) 45 51 96 60

DeSola Group, Inc.
477 Madison Avenue
New York, NY 10022
Tel: 212-832-4770
Fax: 212-371-2135

Gad Shaanan Design
4480 Cote de Liesse
Suite 390
Montreal, Quebec
Canada H4N 2R1
Tel: 514-735-9550
Fax: 514-735-3961

Hartmann & Mehler Designers GMBH
Corneliusstrasse 8
60325 Frankfurt am Main
Tel: 069-756192-0
Fax: 069-746419

Landor Associates
Landor Building
1001 Front Street
San Francisco, CA 94111
Tel: 415-955-1400

Lee Communications, Inc.
11 Conant Valley Road
Pound Ridge, NY 10576
Tel: 914-533-2325

Lippincott & Margulies
499 Park Avenue
New York, NY 10022
Tel: 212 832-3000

Lipson•Alport•Glass & Associates
666 Fifth Avenue
36th Floor
New York, NY 10103
Tel: 212-541-3946
Fax: 212-541-3947

Lloyd Northover
8 Smart's Place
London WC2B 5LW
United Kingdom
Tel: +44 71 430 1100
Fax: +44 71 430 1490

Milton Glaser, Inc.
207 East 32nd Street
New York, NY 10016
Tel: 212-889-3161
Fax: 212-213-4072

Nolin Larosée Design Communications
1470 Peel Street
Building A, Suite 700
Montréal, Québec H3A 1T1
Canada
Tel: 514-499-1331

SampsonTyrrell
6 Mercer St.
London
WC2H 9QA
Tel: +44 (0) 71 379 7124
Contact: Dave Allen, Managing
Director

The Schechter Group, Inc.
437 Madison Avenue
New York, NY 10022
Tel: 212-752-4400

Siegel & Gale
1185 Avenue of the Americas
New York, NY 10036
Tel: 212-730-0101
Fax: 212-730-1462